Stewart, John G.

One last chance

DATE			

ONE LAST CHANCE

One Last Chance

The Democratic Party, 1974–76

JOHN G. STEWART

PRAEGER PUBLISHERS
New York • Washington

Published in the United States of America in 1974
by Praeger Publishers, Inc.
111 Fourth Avenue, New York, N.Y. 10003

© 1974 by Praeger Publishers, Inc.

Library of Congress Catalog Card Number: 73-3678

Printed in the United States of America

To Nancy, Michael, and Cara

PREFACE

This book suggests how the Democratic Party can provide the political leadership that America will need for the balance of this decade and, indeed, the closing decades of this century. The proposition that leadership is now lacking —in both the Democratic and Republican parties—scarcely needs arguing.

Or so it seems as the writer winds up his case. The book was initially conceived in the final weeks of George McGovern's 1972 campaign for the Presidency—when Democratic fortunes had sunk to their lowest level in memory—and written during the spring and summer of 1973 as Watergate unfolded and Republican fortunes can fairly be said to have sunk even lower. Thus the objective conditions facing the Democratic Party changed greatly from the time of the book's conception to its birth: A triumphant Republican President boasting an unprecedented mandate, vigorously assaulting the Democratic Congress on a variety of fundamental political questions, was transformed into an embattled figure principally concerned with salvaging the remnants of his Administration so that he might serve the remaining years of his Presidency with some measure of effectiveness.

The unforeseen developments in the shift of Richard Nixon's personal political fortunes, followed by the resignation of Spiro Agnew and appointment of a new Vice President and the constitutional struggle over executive privilege, forced a much broader focus in the writing than had originally been contemplated. Although the tragedy of Watergate and subsequent events did little to change the basic problems that were facing the Democrats in late 1972 and early 1973, they did make necessary a more thoughtful attempt to assess American politics generally. How was it possible to organize in the United States such a political conspiracy as Watergate revealed? What are the lessons of Watergate and the Agnew affair for the future of democratic government in America and, more specifically, for the Democratic Party? How can these lessons be applied to avoid similar excesses in the future?

The search for answers to these questions took me back in my mind to the evening of January 19, 1961. Washington, D.C., was strangling in the grip of a blizzard of record proportions, measured by the depth of the snow and the numbers of cars abandoned by commuters on their homeward trek. My wife, Nancy, and I leaped into waist-deep drifts on the west terrace of the U.S. Capitol, threw snowballs, and wondered aloud how the inauguration of John F. Kennedy, the nation's thirty-fifth President, could take place the following day.

When the next day dawned clear and very cold, it seemed a great day for Democrats—pristinely appropriate to our faith in Kennedy and our response to his vision of a vibrant and courageous people facing up to the challenges of the post-Eisenhower years. Later we were to witness and participate in other memorable triumphs of the early and mid-1960s—the March on Washington for Jobs and Freedom in 1963, the passage of the Civil Rights Act of 1964, the victory of the Johnson-Humphrey ticket in 1964, and the unprecedented legislative achievements of President Johnson in 1965 and 1966. Anyone who doubts now or doubted then the vitality and responsiveness of the American political system in those years need only review the record of solid accomplishment. The future of the country seemed bright and the Democratic Party's place in that future secure.

But one has also to look back on those early years in Washington with a mixture of great sadness and disappointment. How much went wrong. How naïve we were to believe that the process of democratic government was predictable and tractable. Today, there are moments of great discouragement:

Can the country, let alone the Democratic Party, hope to extricate itself from the wreckage of the past eight years? Can we hope to rebuild the confidence and support of the people that has been squandered so callously by so many people, in so many ways? It is a long way from that magnificent snowy evening behind the Capitol in January 1961.

This book is my attempt to chart the beginning of the way back.

Washington, D.C.
January, 1974   JOHN G. STEWART

ACKNOWLEDGMENTS

How one can adequately acknowledge the many persons who contribute to the writing of a book is, I suppose, a question that authors frequently find hard to answer. It is especially so for this writer. Most of the concerns that motivated me to undertake the book and the insights that shaped it grew out of more than a decade's labors on the staff of the United States Senate, the Office of the Vice President, and the Democratic National Committee. It was my good fortune, in particular, to work with and learn from two of America's most decent and dedicated politicians, Hubert H. Humphrey and Lawrence F. O'Brien. Before that, I spent three exciting years as a graduate student in American politics at the University of Chicago under the tutelage of the late Professor Morton Grodzins, whose understanding of the American federal system informed a generation of scholars and political activists. Above all, the late Professor James A. Storing of Colgate University helped me acquire an enduring belief in the feasibility of democratic government.

That was the background. Additionally, I had specific support and counsel from many persons. In particular, I wish to note the special contribution of Albert H. Cantril. He designed the survey that the Gallup Organization conducted for this book, and he also assembled other data on the state of public opinion. Our conversations helped develop many of the arguments in Chapters 4 and 5, and Chapter 1 draws upon a study of the 1972 presidential campaign he conducted with Charles W. Roll, Jr. Susan Davis Cantril made a number of suggestions in the early stages of the project, and she helped clarify several points in Chapter 6 shortly before the manuscript went to the printer. David Reinhart helped in compiling the research for Chapter 3 on underdog Democrats who won public office in 1972. Judy Aldock and Estelle Keren of the Democratic National Committee's research division were very helpful in checking facts and locating source material.

A number of persons read all or portions of the manuscript. They are appropriately thanked for their substantial help and ritualistically absolved from any responsibility for my errors of fact or interpretation. They include: Douglas J. Bennet, Lynne P. Brown, Mark F. Ferber, Lloyd A. Free, Patricia N. Gray, Robert J. Keefe, Robert W. Nelson, Norman and Virginia Sherman, Alfred L. Stern, and Philip F. Zeidman. A special note of appreciation is due Lois O'Neill, senior editor and director of the Washington office of Praeger Publishers, for her lucid analysis and sharp pencil.

Finally, I thank my wife, Nancy, for her seemingly inexhaustible reservoir of good humor and patience throughout this project. Her criticisms of the manuscript have been constructive and pointed. Her unfailing love has been the one commodity without which the work could never have been completed.

J.G.S.

CONTENTS

ONE LAST CHANCE

1

POLITICS
AND THE
PRESIDENCY

A common thread runs through the presidencies of Eisenhower, Kennedy, Johnson, and Nixon: Each man, using different styles and different methods, sought to liberate his Administration from the constraints of legitimate political debate and the corresponding obligation to recognize and take seriously the often divergent and clashing views that naturally arise as part of the political process. The simple but exceedingly harsh fact that emerged above all others from the excesses of Watergate is that the political disaster of the century—perhaps of American politics for all time—cannot be seen as exclusively the product of the antidemocratic men who served President Nixon, or even as stemming from Richard Nixon's view of his presidential obligations and prerogatives. Watergate and all the broader and pervasive corruption it will forever represent must be seen, by Democrats and Republicans alike, as the most degenerate form of the politics that invested the American Presidency with almost exclusive responsibility for defining the purposes of the nation and consciously derided the importance of nonpresidential political institutions, including the U.S. Congress and the political parties themselves.

It is noteworthy that many of the truly significant political achievements of the recent past—the Trade Expansion Act of 1962, for example, or the Civil Rights Act of 1964, or the Elementary and Secondary Education Act of 1965—occurred in circumstances that *forced* the President to recognize the

complicated politics of the situation and to deal with the opposition through an intricate process of compromise and accommodation. By the same token, the great political tra-
gedies of these years—the Bay of Pigs, the Vietnam War, the
Watergate scandal itself—were, in part, products of a situation
wherein the President insulated himself and the decision-
making process from the clash of divergent interests and
sought to reach highly political decisions without the participation of the nation's political leaders in Congress, in the
states, and in his own party.

We easily fall victim to the myth that the right man—the
right President—can make all the difference in the condition
of our country and the place of our country in the world.
When we invest so much of our attention in the performance
of this one man, we have little left for strengthening our political parties or improving the operations of Congress, for
making our nonpresidential institutions truly responsive to
popular attitudes and beliefs. The consequences are twofold:
The President is installed as the nation's political conscience,
for good or ill, and the institutions that can attend most
directly to the needs of the people are progressively enfeebled.

YEARS OF DECISION

People who live in Washington and try to make sense of
American politics labor under a considerable handicap. Since
few subjects other than politics are ever discussed, and since
relatively few people do most of the talking, it is difficult to
escape from the conventional political wisdom that happens
to be in vogue at a particular time.

As this book was being completed, it was generally thought
that the Democrats—thanks more to the consumer price index
than Watergate—had a good chance to clobber the Republicans in the congressional elections in 1974. This viewpoint
had its irony, to say the least, because six months earlier the
Democratic Party was believed to be in very serious, possibly
fatal, trouble: It had suffered its most stunning presidential

defeat in generations, and President Nixon, wrapped securely in his newly acquired mandate, had launched a frontal assault against Congress to uproot and destroy the Democratic programs and ideology that generally have guided the country since the New Deal. Few people were taking bets against the President.

In many ways, however, the Democratic miseries of late 1972 and early 1973 were little worse than those faced by the Nixon Administration in late 1970 and the first half of 1971. In the aftermath of the 1972 presidential campaign, it was easy to forget that Richard Nixon had been thought to be distinctly vulnerable as the Democrats warmed up for the struggle to select their party's presidential nominee. In both instances—Nixon's troubles in 1970 and 1971 and the widely assumed demise of the Democrats in 1972 and early 1973—Washington's conventional wisdom proved to be short-sighted and short-lived.

Today, political discussion generally focuses on two questions: Will the Democrats be able to capitalize on Nixon's troubles and win a massive victory in 1974? Can the Democrats find a winner for 1976? These are not unimportant questions, to be sure. But, as before, an excessive fascination with the immediate circumstances of political power—who's likely to win or lose the next election—is almost certain to limit, if not obliterate, the serious attention that should be paid to a far more significant story.

To put it directly: 1974 and 1975 have shaped up as years of decision for the Democrats. The party is on the verge of emerging from nearly a decade of the most difficult and divisive internal strife. It is now reasonable to begin talking of a Democratic Party both reformed and united, both open and organized. The passing of the Democrats' long night of discontent, occasioned primarily by the Vietnam War, coincides with a growing perception among party members, arising in part from the lessons of the McGovern campaign, that the appeals and ideology of the New Deal are no longer sufficient for an electorate, or a country, that has changed greatly since the 1930s and 1940s. The McGovern campaign itself dra-

matized the limitations of the New Politics—the activist, antiwar ideology that stressed the common political goals of the
young, the black, the poor, and various intellectual elites.
Finally, the unforeseen problems that erupted around Richard
Nixon in his second term swept away his highly merchan-
dised mandate, giving the Democrats a totally unexpected—
perhaps even undeserved—chance to seize the political initiative.

But there is a great difference for a party between winning
an election—a decidedly short-term proposition—and laying
the ideological and political foundations that can bring electoral success for the next decade or generation. As 1974
loomed, the Grand Old Party was in trouble because of the
economy, Watergate, and the failure of the so-called New
Federalism to deal effectively with the nation's most important domestic problems. But the Democrats were in only
slightly less trouble for 1974 and will be in no better shape
than the GOP for 1976 unless they understand the reasons
for their indifferent, and at times catastrophic, performance
of the past decade, and unless they can go to the American
people with an appeal that is *attractive politically and effective governmentally.*

The choice comes to this: Will the Democrats find the
energy and vision to seize this chance to make the *party* a
significant factor once again in running the country? Or will
1974 and 1975 slip away without the Democrats' facing up
to the basic problems that have plagued their party for more
than a decade and, more importantly, doing something about
them?

Clouding but at the same time giving great urgency to this
choice is the nation's need for fresh and credible evidence
that the American political system can still be made to work.
Whatever proves to be the ultimate outcome of Watergate
and the subsequent struggles over executive privilege and
the prosecution of criminal offenders, we are faced with the
awesome job of putting the pieces together again. *In an environment where politics and politicians are scorned by the
American people as seldom before, the burden of political*

responsibility has never been greater. It is a burden the Democrats cannot escape, however much they might wish otherwise.

We are in a period when many of the fundamental assumptions that have governed American politics since the Depression are in doubt. Party loyalties seem to be weakening; ticket-splitting is more prevalent. Some observers note a sharp decline in political involvement and concern among the electorate, even though educational and income levels are rising. There is much talk about an electorate that is increasingly alienated and cynical about the democratic process itself. But how these changes affect the acquisition and loss of political power, particularly at the national level, is seen only dimly.

This lack of clarity poses a special problem for the Democrats. At the most obvious level, the party has lost the last two presidential elections even though remaining the nominal majority party in Congress. The 1972 presidential results brought an additional bundle of troubles: the emergence of a solid Republican South, a majority of blue-collar workers and Catholics voting for the Republican candidate, a significant portion of Jews abandoning their traditional Democratic allegiance, and, unkindest cut of all, the fact that 33 per cent of the Democrats who voted in 1972 supported Richard Nixon instead of the party's nominee.

The magnitude of George McGovern's defeat raised another basic question: Does the traditional New Deal coalition built by Franklin Roosevelt, if indeed it still exists, possess the strength to send a Democrat to the White House? The Democratic Party's electoral troubles seem rooted in the increasing feebleness of its efforts to appeal to a true majority of the national electorate. This suggests that the Democrats in 1974 must look beyond the voters who are needed for victory in the coming congressional and gubernatorial elections and begin to devise a longer-term strategy for transforming what appears to be a relatively stable congressional majority into a winning presidential coalition. This requires, in turn, a more precise understanding of *who* these voters might be and *how* the party can appeal to them most effectively.

But the Democratic Party's problems run deeper. Internally, the party is still recovering from the self-induced trauma of the Vietnam War and the related effort to achieve greater popular access and participation in the presidential nominating process. The latter, a serious and worthy attempt to bring into the political process a number of people, principally women, blacks, and youth, who had been excluded in the past, was justified by the belief that broader citizen participation and involvement would strengthen the national party by developing a new generation of Democrats who could be added to the New Deal coalition. The reform effort itself, however, further shook the party.

Moreover, the 1972 presidential election raises the possibility that many of the assumptions about the electorate that fueled the reform effort were wrong, even though most of the reforms themselves were constructive and overdue. It at least can be argued that most people don't care very much about personal involvement in the political process and that the activists who do care often display little talent for nominating the candidates or writing the platform that will attract majority support on Election Day. Having bought the argument that participatory democracy was the wave of the future, and then having been crushed by the Nixon landslide, the Democrats cannot escape the difficult job of attempting to discover which aspects, if any, of the reform movement contributed to their defeat and what, if anything, should be done about it. On these crucial matters, two commissions of the Democratic National Committee will make recommendations in 1974 to be implemented in 1975 and 1976.

The problems unique to the Democrats are compounded by the simple fact that the United States itself has changed greatly since the days when FDR stitched together the coalition that was to control American politics for the middle half of the twentieth century. Appeals and solutions that made sense in the context of a given set of economic and social conditions are not necessarily going to work when conditions are totally different. The national Democratic Party is at a point in its history where its purposes and objectives would have to be examined and questioned, even if its failures of 1968 and 1972, the internal strife occasioned by the Vietnam War, and the added strain of the reform crusade had never occurred. The challenge that President Nixon initially leveled against the authority of Congress and the viability of the Democratic Party's notions as to the federal government's role in governing the country cannot be dismissed. Nixon clearly believed that he could eventually prevail in a direct confrontation with Congress over its willingness to continue funding a wide variety of federal programs at levels he considered excessive. Moreover, the initial congressional response to Nixon's challenge—one cast primarily in the rhetoric of the New Deal and the Great Society—left the Democrats very much on the defensive, appearing as opponents of reforming governmental institutions and procedures in light of changing economic and social conditions in the country. The Democrats, for the first time in memory, had donned the mantle of the antichange forces.

Watergate and its consequences, in effect, rescued the Democrats in 1973 from having to devise a more effective counterattack to the Nixon challenge. This temporary reprieve, however, did not remove the basic issues that Nixon raised or eliminate the long-term necessity of a more coherent Democratic response, assuming, that is, a genuine desire by the national party to rebuild its capacity to win the Presidency and then to govern. Nixon at least had a strategy for solidifying his New American Majority and for changing the direction and priorities of the national government. That the execution of these plans assumed a minimum regard for the democratic institutions and constitutional traditions of the country makes it all the more mandatory for the Democrats, as a party, to decide who they are and where they hope to lead the nation.

Can the Democrats do it? That question will dominate American politics in 1974 and 1975, because it is in those years that the issues will be decided, one way or the other, at least in so far as the Democratic *Party* is concerned. By 1976, the year of the presidential nomination and election, the chance for meaningful strengthening of the party will have passed. In the meantime, however, the right decisions in 1974 and 1975—by Congress, at the Democratic National Committee, and in the states—combined with the resounding electoral victory that is now within reach in 1974 can give the Democratic Party a purpose and momentum that have been sorely missing in recent years. What is accomplished in the next two years can lay the foundations for a new Democratic era to begin officially on January 20, 1977, with a Democratic President-elect taking the oath of office on the steps of the U.S. Capitol.

If only a nagging thought could be dismissed: Somehow the Democrats will blow it. Somehow this opportunity to recapture the political leadership of America will be squandered. Democrats, in this regard, would do well to recall the delusive optimism and confidence that overflowed in the aftermath of the 1970 congressional elections.

Controlled fury flashed from Senator Ed Muskie's eyes as he delivered—in measured cadences—the Democratic Party's message on election eve, November 2, 1970. He spoke to the nation from the kitchen of a Republican friend's home in Cape Elizabeth, Maine. The technically perfect color videotape of Muskie's fifteen-minute address had been preceded on the networks by the distinctly imperfect black-and-white videotape of President Nixon's slashing partisan attack delivered several days earlier at an airport rally in Phoenix, Arizona.

It was one of those rare moments in American politics when everything went right. The moment was not to be repeated, either for Ed Muskie or the Democrats, in the next twenty-four months. But that could not have been imagined in the stillness of the Cape Elizabeth kitchen where Muskie, alone in the room but for a single cameraman, talked of the Republican campaign that had featured the rhetorical excesses of both President Nixon and Vice President Spiro T. Agnew.

"They call upon you—the working majority of Americans —to support them while they oppose your interests," Muskie said. "They really believe that if they can make you afraid enough . . . or angry enough . . . you can be tricked into voting against yourself."

Muskie devoted only six words of the speech to an indirect reference to the Vietnam War. Instead, he stressed those issues—inflation, high interest rates, unemployment, reductions in health and education expenditures—that most troubled the traditional Democratic coalition of working Americans. At no point did he criticize the nation or the American people, excepting, of course, those Republicans "from the highest offices in the land" who designed and carried out the GOP's 1970 congressional campaign. In his fifteen minutes, Ed Muskie lifted himself and the Democratic Party into solid contention to recapture the White House two years later.

The next day the 56 million Americans who bothered to vote gave the Democrats additional reasons to feel better about their prospects in 1972:

- a net gain of nine seats in the House of Representatives
- a net loss of two seats in the Senate (but retention of a ten-vote majority) despite a major GOP effort to win control of the chamber
- a net gain of eleven governorships that gave the Democrats a 29–21 Democratic majority in state houses
- 54 per cent of the total congressional vote, compared to 51 per cent in 1968

Much of the Democrats' elation could be explained by their initial fear that Richard Nixon and the Republican Party would do considerably better. Vice President Agnew, alliterating his way from coast to coast, campaigned in twenty-nine states; President Nixon, waiting until the last three weeks before Election Day, still managed to touch down in twenty-three. Both hit hard and repeatedly on what Richard Scammon and Ben Wattenberg have called the "social issue"—crime, violence, permissiveness, drugs and unruly students.

Attractive Republican candidates were recruited to challenge Democratic senators who appeared vulnerable. Indeed, President Nixon himself persuaded twelve incumbent Republican members of the House of Representatives to give up their safe seats to run for the Senate; seven lost. All were provided with ample campaign funds and the most sophisticated campaign support—television, computer letters, polling, advertising—that money could buy. A concerted effort was mounted to capture traditional Democratic blue-collar constituencies—those most attracted by the social issue—and to widen Republican gains in the South.

Most Democrats survived. Of equal significance, most Democrats worked overtime to convince the voters that they, too, were against crime and violence; they, too, opposed student riots and drugs; they, too, believed in the American family, the flag (many wore it on their lapels), and the virtues of hard work. But the Democrats also attacked the Nixon Administration's economic record: the continuing inflation, the rising level of unemployment, the record high interest rates, and the sagging gross national product.

The day after the elections President Nixon strolled out on the lawn at San Clemente to give the press his analysis of the results. He noted that historically the party not controlling the White House has picked up an average of thirty-eight House seats in nonpresidential years. Thus the Democratic gain of only nine House seats could be interpreted as a defeat when compared to the historical average. As for the Senate, Nixon advanced the concept of a "working" or "ideological" majority: "We have increased our majority to a working majority . . . for national defense and also for foreign policy." Not long afterward, Presidential Counselor Robert Finch provided additional insight for the White House press: "Does the loss of governorships by Republicans spell disaster for 1972? Hardly. In 1960, the GOP held only fourteen governorships—yet Vice President Nixon carried twenty-six states. Two major states with Republican governors—New York and Illinois—were lost; two with Democratic governors—California and Ohio—were won."

Nonetheless, the press insisted on writing about the Democratic victory in 1970. In fact, neither party suffered a serious defeat, although the Democrats did considerably better than they had expected to do, given the GOP's well-financed effort to enlarge on Nixon's narrow victory in 1968. After the turmoil of 1968 and the continuing dissension within the Democratic Party, the 1970 elections appeared to signal a rebound in 1972. The party was alive. The basic elements of the Roosevelt coalition had held together. And President Nixon seemed more vulnerable than anyone had expected.

Survey research data from many sources confirmed the existence of an exciting opportunity for a Democratic resurgence in the 1972 presidential election:

Nixon's mediocre job rating as President. In ten out of twelve national polls conducted by the Harris Survey from November 1970 through January 1972, less than a majority of the voters gave Richard Nixon a positive job rating as President. (This includes answers of "excellent" and "pretty good" to the question: "How would you rate the job President Nixon is doing as President—excellent, pretty good, only fair, or poor?")

Nixon's mediocre ratings on specific problems. From mid-1969 through 1971—in eighteen national surveys conducted by Harris—Nixon failed to achieve a single positive rating over 50 per cent in the following areas: handling of Vietnam, crime, law and order, the economy, race and civil rights, taxes, and the cost of living. On the one issue that consistently ranked at or near the top of the listings of the public's major domestic worries and concerns—the cost of living—Nixon's positive job rating frequently fell below 20 per cent.

The country's economic problems. From November 1970 through 1971—on eight successive Harris national surveys—a large majority of the population, usually in excess of two to one, answered this question affirmatively: "Do you feel the country is in a recession today or not?" On the one survey where there was less than a two-to-one spread (January 1971), the affirmatives still swamped the negatives, 56 per cent to

33 per cent, with 11 per cent not sure. Even President Nixon's announcement of his New Economic Policy in August 1971 and the wage-price freeze of Phase I, although generally popular with the public, did not eliminate the economy as a Democratic issue. Harris reported the following changes in the positive ratings given the President between July 1971 and September 1971: "Keeping the economy healthy" rose from 22 per cent in July to 36 per cent in September; "handling taxes and spending" rose from 20 per cent to 28 per cent; "keeping down living costs" rose from 13 per cent to 23 per cent; and "keeping unemployment down" rose from 16 per cent to 21 per cent.

Muskie's good showing in the polls. Following his election eve speech, Ed Muskie assumed the often ill-fated position as the party's "acknowledged front-runner" for the presidential nomination. In this period both the Gallup and Harris polls found Muskie either running ahead of President Nixon or within striking distance in trial heats that included Governor George Wallace. In December 1970, for example, Nixon led Muskie in the Gallup Poll by a single percentage point, 44 per cent to 43 per cent; in February 1972, Nixon's lead was still a single point, 43 per cent to 42 per cent. In the Harris Survey, Muskie spurted to a 46 to 40 per cent lead in November 1970, enlarged his lead to 47 per cent to 39 per cent in April 1971, and in January 1972 was still running even with Nixon, 42 per cent to 42 per cent.

At the start of the presidential year, in other words, the Democrats could take comfort in a better than expected showing in the 1970 congressional elections, a potential challenger running neck and neck with the incumbent President, and the fact that the incumbent minority party President clearly had been unable to meet the public's expectations in almost every policy area, starting with his handling of the Vietnam War and including domestic areas of traditional Democratic strength, such as the economy, as well as problems generally seen as providing an advantage to the Republicans, such as law and order.

Senator George McGovern, in his widely quoted postelection speech at Oxford University, summed up the feeling of most Democrats as they prepared to battle for the party's nomination. He said: "I firmly believed throughout 1971 that the major hurdle to winning the Presidency was winning the Democratic nomination. I believed that any reasonable Democrat could defeat President Nixon."

By late summer 1972, however, it was President Nixon who had seized the initiative in the aftermath of McGovern's extraordinary campaign for his party's nomination. Nixon's political sights had risen: Not only did he expect to win re-election, but he began speaking of a much broader mandate. In his acceptance speech in August 1972 at Miami Beach, Nixon voiced an appeal to a "New American Majority": "I ask you, my fellow Americans, tonight to join us, not in a coalition held together only by a desire to gain power. I ask you to join us as members of a new American majority bound together by our common ideals."

This pitch to the solid majority of non-Republicans in the electorate was little different from Nixon's appeals in 1960 and 1968 "to vote for America"—the only way that an old-line Republican could hope to lure the millions of Democrats and independents needed for victory. One of the more remarkable aspects of the 1972 campaign, however, was McGovern's failure to counter this strategy with an explicit appeal to Democratic loyalties along the lines of Hubert Humphrey in 1968 and John F. Kennedy in 1960. "There is some value in brand names," Kennedy liked to say. "The party labels tell a story of the division between the Republicans and Democrats on the great issues of benefit to our people."

McGovern and the Legacy of 1972

It is this juxtaposition of Nixon's deliberately nonpartisan appeal to a "New American Majority" with the absence of a Democratic counterattack by McGovern that raises an essential question for anyone hoping to decipher the meaning

of the 1972 presidential election returns: Is there, in fact, a
"New American Majority" as defined by Richard Nixon?
And, to take the problem one step farther, does the Nixon
landslide represent a decisive repudiation of the policies and
issues on which the Democratic campaign was based?

According to the votes that were counted on November 7,
1972, it appeared that President Nixon had taken some impressive strides in the direction of his "New American Majority." He had made devastating inroads into strongholds
the Democratic Party had counted on for decades. Over half
(57 per cent) of the blue-collar vote went to Nixon, according
to Gallup Poll measurements before and after the election.
Fifty-one per cent of those with less than a high school
education preferred Nixon, as did 52 per cent of the Catholics.
Even a majority of voters (54 per cent) living in a household
containing a labor union member went for Nixon. And two-
thirds (69 per cent) of the self-proclaimed independents indicated a preference for the incumbent President.

One fact highlights the brutal realities in starkest fashion:
Exactly one-third of the votes cast by Democrats for President
in 1972 were cast for Richard Nixon. In absolute terms, this
amounted to 9.6 million defecting Democrats—a sizable army
to whom the President was more than willing to grant un-
conditional amnesty.

From word and deed it is clear that Richard Nixon, for one,
read his lopsided victory over George McGovern as a ringing
endorsement. Just three weeks after the election, the President
summed it up: "We feel that we have a mandate—a mandate
not simply for approval of what we have done in the past,
but a mandate to continue to provide change that will work."
And soon thereafter he bounded confidently into a confrontation with Congress on a host of controversial matters.

There is evidence to suggest that, even before the Watergate
case broke with full fury, this presidential exuberance was
a serious misreading of what the voters said on November
7. In a special survey commissioned through the Gallup
Organization in mid-October by Albert H. Cantril and Charles
W. Roll, Jr., at the height of the campaign, it was found

that only 37 per cent of the electorate was supporting Nixon out of a belief in him and "what he stands for." The remaining 25 per cent who supported him did so largely because they did not want to see McGovern win. After a national cross-section of registered voters had been asked their preference between the two candidates, they were asked: "Are you supporting the candidate you choose more because you especially like him and what he stands for, or more because you would hate to see the other man win?" [1] Their answers:

TABLE 1

Percentage who:
Support NIXON because

Like him	37
Dislike McGovern	16
A little of both	9

Support McGOVERN because

Like him	18
Dislike Nixon	12
A little of both	8
	100

Thus Richard Nixon's "New American Majority" could not have emerged without a strong assist from George Mc-Govern. Anti-McGovern sentiment (amounting to a firm 16 per cent, joined by 9 per cent who were less than enthusiastic about Nixon) was almost as great as the pro-McGovern sentiment. It was also greater than the anti-Nixon segment of the electorate (12 per cent having a dislike for the President and 8 per cent being qualified in their support).

These figures suggest, in part, why ticket-splitting was so common in 1972. Senator McGovern ran well behind his party. In the thirty-three states where there were Senate races, Nixon achieved a 26-percentage-point margin over McGovern. Republican senatorial candidates, however, accumulated only a 7-point over-all advantage over the Democrats (and, more important, the Democrats scored a net gain of two seats). In only seven of the thirty-three states did Nixon run behind the Republican senatorial candidate, and in all but one of the races the Republican candidate was a liberal: Ted Stevens (Alaska), Charles H. Percy (Illinois), James B. Pearson (Kansas), Edward Brooke (Massachusetts), Clifford P. Case (New Jersey), and Mark Hatfield (Oregon). In the eighteen gubernatorial races, the parties demonstrated equal strength, drawing the same proportion of the popular vote. In the same states at the presidential level, however, McGovern suffered a 24-percentage-point deficit.[2] Thus it was that, in the midst of the Nixon landslide, the Republicans posted a loss of two seats in the Senate, a net loss of one governorship, and the loss of control of two state legislatures. Perhaps some Republicans took solace from the twelve seats gained in the House, but this still left the Democrats with a commanding majority.

The negative influences at work in the 1972 presidential race were illustrated in other ways as well: The voter turnout was the lowest since 1948. Only 55.6 per cent of the potential electorate cast ballots for President, compared to 61.0 per cent in 1968, 62.0 per cent in 1964, and 64.3 per cent when Nixon ran against John Kennedy. In fact, the number of potential voters in 1972 who stayed away from the polls (61.9 million) far exceeded the number of votes received by Richard Nixon (47.2 million).

Richard Nixon's landslide of 1972 thus bears little resemblance to Lyndon Johnson's victory over Barry Goldwater. Although much of Johnson's margin was attributable to a comparable personal rejection of the Arizona Senator, LBJ's strength in 1964—and the strength of the Democratic Party generally—carried the Democrats to a gain of two seats in the Senate, thirty-eight seats in the House, and a net gain in Democratic control of eighteen state legislatures. Lyndon Johnson's coattails were cut from Texas cloth—long, broad, and all-enveloping.

Although the voters rejected George McGovern—the presidential candidate—in 1972, it would be wrong to interpret his personal rejection as an equally definitive rejection of all of the concerns he articulated in the course of his campaign. With the exception of his well-publicized, although

changing, stands on such issues as amnesty, abortion, and welfare reform, surprising public support existed for certain of
the positions McGovern took.

Evidence of support for the Senator's stand on major issues
was found in the mid-October survey by Cantril and Roll
referred to earlier. Four key issues were singled out on which
Nixon and McGovern were clearly divided. Without referring
to the candidates by name, the contending views of the two
men were juxtaposed and respondents were asked which way
they "leaned" (see Table 2). On the matter of wage and
price controls, a majority agreed with McGovern's contention
that they were not fair. A plurality of opinion sided with
McGovern's position that the way to hold down taxes was
not to cut back on federal spending but to close the tax loopholes. Only a narrow plurality agreed with Nixon's complaint
in Miami Beach that "it has become fashionable in recent
years to point up what is wrong with what is called the
American system." Even the controversial issue of cutbacks in
defense spending found two in five agreeing with the Mc-
Govern stand.

TABLE 2

Percentage Responding:

WAGE AND PRICE CONTROLS	Wage and price controls have not worked because they are not tough enough on profits of corporations.	57
	Wage and price controls have begun to slow down the rising cost of living and are fair.	29
	No opinion.	14
		100
TAXES	The most important way to keep down the taxes of the average taxpayer is to make the large corporations and wealthy people assume a greater part of the tax burden.	43
	The most important way to keep down the taxes of the average taxpayer is to slow down spending for government programs.	35
	Both.	14
	No opinion.	8
		100

TABLE 2 (continued)

TONE OF NATIONAL LIFE	Not enough attention is being paid to those things that are not working right in the U.S. today.	42
	There is too much talk about those things that are not working right in the U.S. today.	47
	No opinion.	11
		100
DEFENSE SPENDING	We are spending more money on military defense programs than is necessary and we can cut back considerably on defense programs over the next few years without weakening our national security.	39
	Any further cuts in our defense spending would dangerously weaken our national security.	48
	No opinion.	13
		100

What, then, was the problem, given this public support for much of what McGovern stood for? Cantril and Roll argue that the Senator's poor showing reflected the fact that he did not appear "presidential" to the American people. Nor was he able to engage the public's trust—the essential ingredient for success in presidential politics.

In a poll conducted for *Newsweek* by the Gallup Organization in mid-August 1972, a cross-section of the public was shown a list of words and phrases and asked to select those that best described each candidate. Consistently, McGovern compared unfavorably to Nixon in those personal attributes associated with the Presidency. For example, the phrase "sticks to principles" was selected by 40 per cent as applying to Nixon and by only 17 per cent as describing McGovern. The phrase "strong and forceful" drew 34 per cent for Nixon and only 17 per cent for McGovern. "Good judgment" was chosen by 30 per cent as applying to the President and by only 11 per cent as applying to Senator McGovern. On the negative side, the phrase "extremist" was pinned on McGovern by 20 per cent as against only 3 per cent for Nixon; 18 per cent felt McGovern "makes snap decisions" in contrast to only 9 per cent for Nixon.

The depth of the irony in the public's perception of Mc-Govern was found in another survey conducted by Cantril in late August that revealed a view of Nixon as better able to handle even those focal campaign issues that McGovern had tried to carve out for himself.[3] For example, when it came to the problem of "making the government pay more attention to the problems of the working man and his family," 61 per cent of the public expressed considerable confidence in Nixon in comparison to only 43 per cent for McGovern. McGovern said, "Come home, America, from the entrenchment of special privilege." Again, McGovern compared unfavorably in the survey: More than half (52 per cent) expressed confidence in Nixon on the matter of "keeping the big interests from having too much influence over the government," as against only 35 per cent expressing confidence in McGovern. Even the job of "reducing unemployment"—surely an issue on which a Democratic candidate should receive a more favorable rating—was not exempt from this pattern: 50 per cent had confidence in Nixon and only 35 per cent in McGovern.

The data make it difficult for anyone who likes Senator McGovern and who admired his refusal to give up at any point in the 1972 campaign to avoid a distinctly unhappy conclusion. The voters' rejection of McGovern was, at base, a personal one. They concluded that he lacked the qualities needed to carry out the duties of President. But little happened in the campaign itself to heal the ideological schisms within the Democratic Party, and a great deal happened to make it relatively easy for the Republican opposition to exploit certain of McGovern's more controversial proposals, such as welfare reform and reductions in the defense budget.

Other volumes have examined in detail a number of incidents that contributed to the McGovern collapse. The California debates with Humphrey, the Eagleton controversy, Pierre Salinger's mission to Paris to negotiate with the North Vietnamese, and the ill-starred welfare reform proposal, for example, have been probed and picked apart by many writers.

But what exactly are the lessons of the McGovern campaign that can help the Democrats understand more clearly where they should go and what they should do between now and 1976? This is the question that matters now.

The McGovern strategists, first of all, forgot the wisdom of V. O. Key, Jr., in his book *The Responsible Electorate:*

> Voters may reject what they have known; or they may approve what they have known. They are not likely to be attracted in great numbers by promises of the novel or unknown. . . . The opposition can maximize its strength as it centers its fire on those elements of the Administration program disliked by the largest numbers of people. Thus, as a matter of practical politics, it must appear to be a common scold rather than a bold exponent of innovation.[4]

How off the mark McGovern was in his acceptance speech in Miami Beach when he said: "We are entering a new period of important, hopeful change in America comparable to the political ferment released in the eras of Jefferson, Jackson and Roosevelt. . . . So let our opponents stand on the *status quo,* while we seek to refresh the American spirit. . . . We are not content with things as they are. We reject the view of those who say: 'America—love it or leave it.' We reply: 'Let us change it so we can love it the more.' " To a public cherishing its sense of accomplishment at the personal level—a well-documented finding—no words stir greater doubt and misgivings than "change" or "political ferment," especially when they are spoken by a man already perceived by many voters as a radical or extremist.[5]

This sense of personal accomplishment among most voters should have suggested the difficulty of mobilizing public concern over specific national problems until these problems were seen as impinging in a direct way on an individual's ability to provide for his future and the well-being of his family. A special survey by Cantril conducted in May 1972 showed that the two most vulnerable spots in the Nixon record were crime and the rising cost of living. These two issues stood out —even among the President's own supporters—as being of preeminent national importance, and both had the potential for strong personal impact on the voters. Most significantly, both were issues on which President Nixon was judged as not doing an acceptable job.

McGovern supporters can point to an impressive stack of speeches and position papers as evidence that the Senator really did zero in on these Nixon vulnerabilities. But this effort, in turn, was undermined by two other factors: (1) McGovern's inability to *sustain* an attack against Nixon's record in areas of his greatest vulnerability: the cost of living, crime, and, to a lesser degree, taxes; and (2) Nixon's success in keeping McGovern on the defensive—and therefore constantly explaining his "real" position—on welfare, defense, and the "three As": amnesty, abortion, and acid. What would start out one week as a spirited and hard-hitting attack by McGovern against rising prices would, by mid-week, be diverted into a renewed effort to criticize the President's handling of the Vietnam War or the immorality and corruption of the Nixon Administration, concerns that lacked the direct personal tie to the interests of the average voter. Thus the initial attempt to exploit a significant Nixon weakness would be almost completely vitiated.

The point here is McGovern's lack of clarity about the need to establish a direct linkage between the major vulnerabilities in Nixon's domestic record and the individual voter's ability to sustain a feeling of personal accomplishment in Nixon's second term. The strategy and issues that carried McGovern to the nomination were not sufficient to produce a victory in the general election. The postconvention campaign was little more than an extension of his preconvention effort, punctuated occasionally by bursts of activity designed to win back defecting Democrats and broaden the candidate's base of support.

President Nixon's strongest suit was in foreign affairs. The draft had been ended; U.S. troop strength in Vietnam was at its lowest level since the early 1960s; the SALT agreements had been signed; and the public was still captivated by the Peking and Moscow trips. Yet it was here that McGovern spent an inordinate amount of effort. He seemed unable to shake his all-consuming concern with the war and its impact

on national priorities, even though every scrap of survey research indicated that this continued emphasis was shutting
off whatever chance he had to fashion a winning presidential
coalition. This situation was compounded by the fact that
McGovern's eloquence and commitment were most visible
when he talked about the war and its impact on America. He
was, in short, most effective on those issues that had the least
political mileage and least effective on those issues that had
the most mileage in terms of winning the Presidency.

Had the McGovern campaign been more aggressive and
imaginative in its criticism of the Nixon domestic record, the
principal issue of the campaign could have become the ade-
quacy of Nixon's stewardship during his first term—how well
Nixon was meeting the needs of the average American family.
Instead, the combination of McGovern's emphasis on Nixon's
strongest issues and his persistence in offering detailed and
controversial proposals on the domestic front, without first
establishing Nixon's vulnerabilities in these areas, resulted in
McGovern himself, rather than the domestic failures of the
first four Nixon years, becoming the principal issue.

One of the propositions propounded by the New Politics
is that the system is rigged against the average citizen. "Alienation" early became a byword in the McGovern campaign
—an all-inclusive term to capture the sense of public frustration and outrage at how little influence "the people" have
over the events shaped by the institutions running their
lives. Out of this grew McGovern's particular brand of populism.

There is little doubt that the public is feeling increasingly
isolated from government. In studies done by the Survey
Research Center of the University of Michigan the trend has
been clearly documented. For example, in 1964 nearly two-
thirds of the public felt that government was run for the
benefit of all the people. By 1970 the figure had dropped to
41 per cent. Over this same six-year period, public feeling
that the government in Washington can be trusted to do
what is right at least most of the time dropped from 77 to 54
per cent (see Table 3).[6] The trend has intensified.

TABLE 3

	1964	1966	1968	1970
Would you say the government is pretty much run:	*Percentage answering "yes":*			
by a few big interests looking out for themselves?	29	34	39	50
for the benefit of all the people?	64	53	52	41
by both? It depends?	4	6	5	5
Don't know.	3	7	4	4
How much of the time do you think you can trust the government in Washington to do what is right?	*Percentage answering:*			
Just about always.	14	17	8	7
Most of the time.	63	48	53	47
Only some of the time.	22	31	37	44
Don't know.	1	4	2	2

Other evidence shows that this mood of cynicism and alienation persisted well into 1972. A May survey by Cantril showed that 78 per cent of the public agreed that "the big special interests in this country have too much power and pretty much have their own way." Seventy-two per cent agreed that "too few of our nation's leaders understand what the average citizen would like to see done in this country." And further, 60 per cent agreed with the proposition that "there is not very much the average citizen can do to influence the way things are going in this country." [7]

At first glance, it would appear that McGovern's playing on these themes could not but work to his advantage in the presidential campaign. His essentially populist appeal had worked reasonably well in the primaries—at least until California. However, the sentiments embodied in these statements of alienation were *not* confined to McGovern's turf alone— not uniquely associated with those in the electorate preferring McGovern over Nixon or Governor Wallace. As Table 4 shows, large majorities of those supporting Nixon and Wallace also shared these views.

Or, to array these same survey findings in another manner, only 32 per cent of those agreeing that the special interests have too much power preferred McGovern over either Nixon or Wallace. As regards those feeling that there is not much the average citizen can do to influence events, 30 per cent selected McGovern. And among those feeling that too few of our nation's leaders understand what people would like to see done, McGovern was the candidate of only 32 per cent.

TABLE 4

	Percentage Agreeing Among Supporters of:		
	Nixon	Wallace	McGovern
The big special interests in this country have too much power and pretty much have their own way.	73	81	85
Too few of our nation's leaders understand what the average citizen would like to see done in this country.	70	77	74
There is not very much the average citizen can do to influence the way things are going in this country.	55	69	62

The McGovern campaign read only half the signs of the public's mood of alienation and cynicism. Approached in another manner in the same May survey, the public was shown to have some fundamental misgivings with respect to racial matters and the whole question of "permissiveness." Specifically, 84 per cent in the survey agreed with the statement: "There has been a breakdown in the respect for authority and the way things have traditionally been done in this country, and many young people have gotten out of hand." Two-thirds (69 per cent) agreed that "blacks and people in other minorities expect things to improve too quickly and are making unreasonable demands."

Surprisingly, a majority of even McGovern's supporters agreed with both of these statements—three-fourths in the matter of a breakdown in respect for authority. As might be expected, supporters of Nixon and Wallace agreed more often than McGovern partisans with these more hard-line views (see Table 5). Nonetheless, the bulk of McGovern's support also was in agreement.

TABLE 5

| | *Percentage Agreeing Among Supporters of:* | | |
	Nixon	Wallace	McGovern
There has been a breakdown in the respect for authority and the way things have traditionally been done in this country, and many young people have gotten out of hand.	87	91	77
Blacks and people in other minorities expect things to improve too quickly and are making unreasonable demands.	75	82	57

Thus there were two types of cynicism manifest as the presidential campaign began to pick up speed—two ways of being "turned off" at the way things were going. At first glance it might be assumed that a "cynicism of the right" could be differentiated from a "cynicism of the left." [8] That is, one segment of the electorate could be singled out that felt the system is stacked against the common man; another segment could be characterized by "hard hat" toughness on the matter of race and permissiveness. Importantly, however, these two distinct sentiments of cynicism were not associated in any simple fashion with two distinct opposing segments of the electorate. Many observers seem to have glossed over the fact that these seemingly inconsistent sentiments were perfectly compatible in the minds of the vast majority of the voters. It was not just a matter of confrontation between New York construction workers and students protesting the war. Thus any candidate in 1972 who looked to voter cynicism toward government and special interests as a weapon in his campaign had to find a way to separate these concerns from the equally potent feelings among the electorate concerning permissiveness and race. The outcome of the presidential contest suggests that McGovern never found the answer.

McGovern's problems were far from simple. Once a sizable portion of the electorate came to believe he lacked the capacity to execute the duties of a President. But little took place in the campaign itself to allay this concern or to rally the basic Democratic strength that the party's nominee should expect to receive.

Whether without the Eagleton affair the situation would have been less disastrous cannot ever be known. But certainly much of the problem can be traced to a lack of perception on the part of McGovern and his preconvention staff as to the differences between the ideological demands of winning the Democratic Party's presidential nomination and of winning the Presidency itself. As Gary Hart has made clear in *Right from the Start: A Chronicle of the McGovern Campaign,* considerable time was invested in planning the financial and organizational activities for the general election.[9] But when it came to issues, to the all-important posture that McGovern would assume after the convention, there is no evidence of any serious effort to think through or implement the ideological requirements of attracting the kind of coalition that was essential to win the White House.

How else explain the McGovern spot commercials that received extensive exposure after Labor Day? The setting became familiar: McGovern in casual attire, surrounded by a small gathering of factory workers, homeowners, or wounded Vietnam veterans, projecting his concerns for the problems of the average citizen, or just listening to their complaints. The informality probably came across to the viewers as contrived and certainly did little to bolster McGovern's sagging image as a potential President. What is he doing in a factory, with his coat off, arguing with blue-collar workers? Once McGovern's credibility as President became the campaign's central issue, his repeated exposure in the same commercials only reinforced this critical weakness and made it more difficult to shift the public's attention to the known vulnerabilities of President Nixon.

The same commercials had worked successfully in the primaries, when the goal was quite different: to differentiate McGovern from a pack of more traditional Democrats competing for the nomination. But once the nomination was in hand, it is hard to understand the failure to link McGovern to the Democratic Party in his postconvention commercials. After some pointed objections from National Campaign Chairman Lawrence F. O'Brien, the tag line on the McGovern commercials was changed from "McGovern . . . for the people" to "McGovern . . . Democrat . . . for the people." But the spots in their substance never made this point effectively, nor did they dramatize the obvious domestic weaknesses of the Nixon record in a manner that attracted the attention of traditional Democrats. The spots, in other words, never spelled out the consequences of "four more years" for the average working family, or anyone else, even though the exploitation of Nixon's mediocre domestic record offered McGovern his best chance to regain a measure of political initiative.

In contrast, the Nixon campaign's decision to "re-elect the President" was extremely shrewd in that it reinforced the significant advantage he already possessed in the presidential image department and simultaneously played down the President's ties to the Republican Party. Richard Nixon understood, even if George McGovern seemingly did not, that an election decided along party lines would be a losing effort for the Republicans. He therefore made it as painless as possible for disgruntled Democrats to support his candidacy. The success of this effort is best illustrated by the phrase "Democrats for *Nixon*," which became firmly established in the public's mind by Election Day. Equally effective were the Nixon commercials that attacked the details of McGovern's controversial defense and welfare proposals, keeping McGovern on the defensive and deflecting sustained public attention away from the weak points in the Nixon record. On the basis of the spot commercials of the respective campaigns, one might have concluded that Nixon was the challenger and McGovern the incumbent.

McGovern blamed his massive defeat on the Wallace voters who allegedly moved *en masse* to support Nixon in the absence of a Wallace third-party candidacy. But, as this analysis has suggested, McGovern did almost nothing to attract their support by a sustained criticism of the Nixon domestic record in, for example, controlling crime or lowering consumer prices, or by effectively separating his populist message—jobs, tax reform, antibigness, anticorporations—from a host of controversial social proposals that diverted the public's attention from the more basic Democratic issues.

What are the principal lessons for the future of the Democratic Party?

First, it can be said that, even before the surfacing of the Watergate conspiracy or the collapse of Phase III price controls, President Nixon's claim of a decisive mandate flowing from the 1972 election was overdrawn. This fact should strengthen the Democratic Congress in responding to the President's efforts to dismantle in wholesale fashion the existing federal structure for handling domestic problems and his related offensive to undermine the authority and power of the legislative branch. But it does not relieve the Democrats themselves of the burden of carrying forward the most searching and critical analysis of the ideological assumptions left over from the New Deal as to the most effective way to attack contemporary domestic problems. There exists today a real opportunity for the Democrats in Congress to begin evolving a more effective federal role in a manner that remains faithful to the Democratic Party's traditional concern for people and their problems, for social justice, and for human rights. Their energies do not have to be devoted totally to defending the barricades against the Nixon assault.

Second, on the presidential side, as 1976 looms, Democrats must remember what happens when a candidate for office, or an incumbent governmental official, fails to connect the processes of politics and government to the alleviation of concerns that people encounter in their daily lives. Primarily because of his own problems of credibility, McGovern never forged this link successfully in 1972. His campaign suffered accordingly. Nor could McGovern convince enough voters that four more years of the Nixon Administration would jeopardize their sense of well-being and accomplishment, even though a majority were clearly dissatisfied with Nixon's domestic record. The public's feelings of alienation toward the impersonality, corruption, and unresponsiveness of government cannot be overcome by political appeals, however well-intentioned, that appear to threaten economic or social stability. Moral outrage is still not an acceptable substitute for common sense in most American homes.

If this analysis has been critical of the McGovern campaign, the data and the conduct of the campaign itself make such criticism mandatory. But it is equally important to emphasize two very significant contributions made by McGovern to the Democratic Party's future.

First, the McGovern campaign demonstrated the feasibility of relying upon small contributors for a substantial proportion of the money needed to run a national political campaign. Gary Hart reports in his book that an estimated total of 1.2 million people—at the national and state levels—contributed $16,750,000 in the postconvention period, a truly remarkable achievement. Even if the 1976 presidential campaign cannot be conducted with public funds—an issue that remains undecided at this writing—McGovern's success should prove the possibility of relying on small contributors to support much of the year-round activities of the Democratic Party and in financing congressional and gubernatorial campaigns. The essential precondition, as McGovern partisans are quick to point out, is to reach the potential contributors with an appeal that truly motivates them to give.

The McGovern campaign can also be seen as the final act in the bitter internal tragedy played out within the Democratic Party between the initial escalation in Vietnam in 1965 and the Miami Beach convention in 1972. In 1968, the traditional Democrats controlled the party and lost the Presidency. In 1972, the advocates of the New Politics carried the day and lost the Presidency. Most fair-minded observers now conclude from these two experiences that only a Democratic Party both open and unified has any realistic hope of winning next time around. Both sides, which battled so viciously in these years, ought now to recognize that neither has an absolute claim on virtue or wisdom, that the moral certainty of their respective positions is subject to all the limits and ambiguities of human experience. The very magnitude of McGovern's defeat fortunately helped to reduce natural tendencies toward recrimination and toward blaming anti-McGovern forces for the loss, which might have occurred if Nixon had won in 1972 by the narrow margin of 1968.[10]

Since 1965 the Democratic Party has changed greatly. The McGovern campaign, to its everlasting credit, brought in a new generation of highly committed and courageous workers, most of whom give every sign of remaining within the party and working for its future success. The internal reforms that many persons believed impossible to achieve have been adopted and carried out. Chapter 2 is devoted to a fuller understanding of these reforms—the successes that should be preserved and the failures that should be remedied.

TAKING POLITICS SERIOUSLY

It was hardly surprising to read George Gallup's report released during the Watergate inquiry that "it is doubtful that at any time in this century politics has commanded so little respect. A key contributing factor has undoubtedly been Watergate." But this decline in public confidence had been under way for some time, years before Watergate blanketed the nation's newspapers and television screens. Surely it is due less to the discovery of massive corruption at the White House level than to the fact that political institutions, at all levels, no longer seem to be working effectively. Despite convincing, and at times dramatic, displays of presidential leadership, concrete results are often meager, leaving the public dismayed over the seeming impotence of our political institutions and confused over whom to hold responsible.

It is clear that we can no longer afford to concern ourselves solely with the *ends* of government, however laudatory and noble these ends may appear. We have learned the hard way that it is time to lower our sights to the more mundane and unexciting business of worrying about the *means* of government—how decisions are made and how promises are carried out. Improved mechanisms are needed for dealing honestly and directly with a host of governmental problems that affect the kinds of lives Americans are able to live. This means taking the politics of the country seriously.

A revitalized and responsive political system—anchored in two strong national parties—is the best and probably the only way to begin rebuilding the public's faith in the governmental process without sacrificing fundamental democratic freedoms. Clinton Rossiter once said, "No America without democracy, no democracy without politics, no politics without parties, no parties without compromise and moderation." Yet even if one agrees with Rossiter's proposition, our present dilemma is as tough as it is obvious: How can public confidence in the American system be revitalized through political institutions that caused much of the decline of confidence in the first place?

David S. Broder, in his 1972 book *The Party's Over,* handed down the basic indictment:

> My view is that American politics is at an impasse, that we have been spinning our wheels for a long, long time; and that we are going to dig ourselves ever deeper into trouble, unless we find a way to develop some political traction and move again. I believe that we can get that traction, we can make government responsible and responsive again, only when we begin to use the political parties as they are meant to be used.

For Broder, and others, this means moving "toward a more responsible two-party system," to borrow the title of the still frequently cited report, released in 1950, of the committee on political parties of the American Political Science Association. In essence, the "responsible-party" argument calls for a greater commitment by the national parties to a specific ideology and agenda of programs that, in turn, would give the voters a decisive choice at election time. It also calls for the majority party's possession and exercise of internal mechanisms and discipline, once in power, to see its program enacted into law. This kind of more rational and responsible party system, the argument runs, would provide a badly needed sense of direction and would eliminate the obstacles and stalemates that have kept our elected leaders from dealing effectively with urgent public problems. Some of the more ardent responsible-party advocates—not Broder, to be sure—even lapse into emotional appeals to abandon the Constitution in favor of a parliamentary system of some sort, believing that such a system would be more hospitable to such disciplined parties.

This is not the place to debate in detail the merits of the responsible-party argument—that exercise has already filled a goodly number of scholarly volumes and learned journals—but it should be noted that much of the argument misses the point of our present difficulties. Truly responsible parties would require authority at the national party level to control, at a minimum, the nomination of candidates for the U.S. House and Senate. A party member who defied the national leadership on critical issues would then face the ultimate sanction: denial of the party's nomination for his or her seat in Congress. Such action would undoubtedly improve party discipline, but it would seriously limit the degree to which an individual party member could represent the unique views of his or her constituents. And restoration of confidence in the American political system requires, above all, a more direct and visible link between the actions and decisions of elected officials and the attitudes and beliefs of their constituents.

The entire American political tradition is founded on the notion of parties organized from the bottom up, with power anchored firmly in local interests, concerns, and personalities. The solution to our problems, therefore, does not lie in abandoning a political system that has existed for nearly two centuries; it lies in building new awareness of the positive attributes that can flow from decentralized political power organized in the two loosely structured and, at times, overlapping national coalitions that we call political parties.

Historically, the strong local orientation of the national parties has given the states and regions of our continental nation a voice in the development of national policies. The absence of power to expel obstreperous party members forced a process of accommodation and compromise in the development of national policies that, in most instances, protected the interests of a clear majority of Americans on most vital issues. There were tmies, regrettably, when the system faltered —an example being the decades that were needed to enact effective civil rights legislation. But the larger historical record is one of achieving a fairly workable balance between progress and stability.

Our present condition calls for not a wholesale dismemberment of the Constitution with the goal of increasing power at the national level under the rubric of a more responsible party system—a development that inevitably could only expand the President's domain—but, instead, a number of less dramatic steps that, taken together, would achieve a more equitable balance between presidential leadership in policymaking and the diverse attitudes represented in our two major parties, especially as these attitudes are expressed in Congress. It is a matter of letting the parties in Congress, in their diversity, assume a larger measure of direct responsibility for governing the country.

To be sure, the Presidency remains pivotal in exercising effective governing power; but presidential power, for all its majesty, must be leavened by the clash of interests and values found on Capitol Hill and across the country. The choice is not between a blind subservience to presidential initiatives and the mindless chaos of 535 individual members of Congress acting independently of all direction. There is a midpoint that represents American politics at its best: vigorous presidential leadership confronted by congressional spokesmen who bring significant expertise and perspective to the public dialogue. But this balance requires informed and active congressional leaders, as well as vastly strengthened political parties in the states.

The decline of public confidence in political institutions is rooted in the fact that these institutions are no longer perceived as adequately meeting the needs of many different kinds and classes of Americans. Thus the parties *in Congress and the states,* if they are to be taken seriously by the Presi-

dent or anyone else, must address themselves in a more coherent fashion to real problems, and they must assume
greater responsibility to see that solutions are carried out.

One unfortunate side effect of the Watergate scandal has
been a heightening of the level of Washington gossip concerning the identity of the Democratic Party's presidential
nominee in 1976. Is Teddy really in the race? Can he win?
What about Scoop Jackson? And Muskie? What is Governor
Wallace up to? Is Mondale serious? This chatter confirms
that many people who ought to know better still subscribe to
the magical theory of presidential salvation. Everything can
be made right again if only the Democrats (or the Republicans) settle on a winning candidate. Yet no single Democrat
(or Republican), however magical, can offer us either the wisdom to know what is right for the country or the political
skill to achieve it.

Governing a republic is not that easy. Nor, for that matter,
is winning an election.

2

THE REFORM
IMPERATIVE

The years of disintegration of the Democratic Party's majority presidential coalition have coincided, in large measure, with the party's efforts to open doors to a constituency even broader than FDR's. The reform agenda that commanded priority attention within the party from 1969 to 1972 was justified, at least in part, as being the most reliable way to recruit a new generation of Democrats, thereby ensuring the party's majority status in the closing decades of the century.

But if one takes the presidential returns of 1972 at face value, it is not off the mark to conclude that years of dedicated effort to open the Democratic Party to a broader constituency ended with the largest exodus of Democrats in generations. One is even tempted to suggest that, if the party opens its doors any further, it might vanish completely.

It is, of course, neither that simple nor that obvious. The Democratic presidential coalition, for example, has been in trouble for many years. But it is equally necessary to recognize the coincidence between the achievement of significant internal reforms and the massive defections of traditional Democrats in the contest for the Presidency. If the party seriously intends to build a winning presidential coalition in 1976 and subsequent elections, it cannot avoid taking a hard look at the motivation, ideology, and consequences of party reform. This, in turn, means a hard look at the impact of the Vietnam War on the party's actions and decisions for the past decade. For the frustrated antiwar activism of the late 1960s was the seedbed of the "New Politics" that ultimately failed in the 1972 general election.

REALITY OF REFORM

Social critics who specialize in wringing their hands about the imperviousness to change of American institutions should be mightily puzzled by what has been taking place within the national Democratic Party for the past eight years. The cynical assumption that powerful political leaders would never permit any dilution of their authority and control is contradicted by the facts. Whether one looks at the written rules and procedures that governed the Democratic presidential nominating process in 1972 or at the delegates who were chosen by the process, the evidence of decisive change is clear and unmistakable.

At the 1968 Democratic National Convention, for example, women comprised 13 per cent of the delegates, blacks 5.5 per cent and youth (under thirty-one) 3 per cent; 67 per cent of the 1968 delegates were attending their first convention. In 1972, following the promulgation and implementation of the delegate-selection reforms, the percentages of blacks and women attending the Democratic National Convention in Miami Beach nearly tripled and the percentage of young delegates increased more than five times. Women accounted for 40 per cent of the delegates, blacks 15 per cent, young people 24 per cent, and 83 per cent of the 1972 delegates were attending their first national convention.

The incidence of change can be illustrated in other ways: Lawyers provided 30 per cent of the delegates in 1968 but only 12 per cent in 1972. In fact, *housewives* were the largest occupational group at the 1972 Democratic National Convention (369 delegates), followed by lawyers (360), teachers (346), and government officials (288). Officeholders, however, were fewer in number: In 1968, twenty-three out of twenty-five Democratic governors were delegates at Chicago; in 1972, only nineteen out of thirty made it to Miami Beach. Two-thirds of the Democrats in the U.S. Senate were delegates in 1968, but this fell to less than one-third in 1972.

In 1968, nearly 13 per cent of the delegates were selected by committees of party officials, the procedure most removed from the influence of rank-and-file Democrats. Even though the reformed rules permitted a maximum of 10 per cent of a state delegation in 1972 to be selected by party committees, only 1.7 per cent of the delegates were actually selected in this manner. To put it another way, 98.3 per cent of the delegates to the 1972 convention were elected by primary or open caucus or convention procedures. Whether or not these changes were beneficial in every respect will be considered later, but there can be little argument that important changes did, in fact, occur.[1]

The most fundamental change of all took place on February 19, 1971, when the Democratic National Committee adopted the eighteen guidelines for delegate selection originally promulgated by the Commission on Party Structure and Delegate Selection (the McGovern-Fraser Commission) and included them as part of the Preliminary Call for the 1972 Democratic National Convention. By establishing specific procedural criteria that state Democratic parties would have to meet in choosing delegates for the national convention, the national party achieved an unprecedented degree of control over the actions of state parties. Although the guidelines acknowledged that delegate-selection procedures could vary from state to state, the imposition of minimum standards in the operation of these procedures forced every state party to make significant changes in rules, traditions, and, in some instances, state law.

The reforms were not limited to the procedures for selecting the delegates who would go to Miami Beach. A second Democratic Party commission, the Commission on Rules, recommended an equally comprehensive set of changes in the organization and conduct of the national convention itself. The commission's chairman, Republican James O'Hara of Michigan, set the tone at the first meeting: "We have the right and duty to turn things upside down, around or sideways if by so doing we will ensure the kind of participation in party affairs toward which we are striving."[2]

Democratic National Chairman Lawrence F. O'Brien

summed up the national party's commitment to its reform
agenda at the conclusion of a Democratic National Committee meeting in October 1971: "We have steadfastly maintained
the course charted by the 1968 National Convention in the
area of party reform. We have taken the '68 mandate and implemented it. . . . Never has a political party so totally
changed its way of doing business in such a short period of
time. . . . And there will be no turning back."

The reality of reform in the delegate-selection process and
in the operation of the national convention itself makes it
more necessary to find specific answers to one critical question: How could the Democrats do so many of the "right"
things—as defined by an impressive collection of political
commentators and practitioners—and end up so poorly on
Election Day? Perhaps no question is more central to the
Democratic search for a presidential majority to match the
party's continuing successes in Congress and in gubernatorial
and state legislative contests.

ORIGINS OF REFORM

The great leap forward in Democratic Party reform took
place between 1969 and the 1972 Democratic National Convention, a direct outgrowth of the bitter and divisive struggle
for the party's presidential nomination in 1968 and the dis-
unity that plagued Hubert Humphrey through the general
election campaign. But these steps can be more clearly understood—and their strengths and shortcomings more accurately
evaluated—if they are viewed as part of a reform process that
has been gaining momentum with the Democratic Party
throughout the entire post-Roosevelt era.

The issue that dominated the pre-1968 Democratic conventions, apart from the quadrennial battle for the presidential nomination, was, of course, civil rights. At times the issue
arose in the context of the platform, as in 1948, when adoption of the minority civil rights plank resulted in a mass exodus of Southern delegations and the creation of the Dixiecrat
ticket in the general election. At other times, such as the 1952
convention, the issue remained in the background but was

nonetheless at the root of the "loyalty oath" controversies in which the Northern and Western wings of the party attempted to compel Southern delegates to pledge their support of the Democratic ticket in the presidential campaign.

In those earlier conventions, however, the split over civil rights never led the national party to question the procedures followed by the state parties in selecting their national convention delegates. It was simply a matter of securing the loyalty to the national ticket of those Southern delegates who were chosen.

This pattern changed abruptly in 1964. At Atlantic City a group of Mississippi Democrats, predominantly black and loyal to the national party, challenged the credentials of the regular Mississippi delegation on the basis of alleged discrimination and exclusion in the delegate-selection process. At a convention where the only other item of undecided business was President Lyndon Johnson's selection of his running mate, the Mississippi Freedom Democratic Party's challenge dominated the nation's television screens and raised the possibility of a Southern walkout if credentials were denied to the regular Mississippi delegation. Needless to say, the prospect of a split convention did not exactly match President Johnson's expectations of what the delegates in Atlantic City were supposed to be doing.

The moving testimony of Fanny Lou Hamer and other Mississippi Democrats before the Credentials Committee left little doubt of the intimidation, violence, and outrageous procedures that had been used systematically to deny their participation in the delegate-selection process. At the same time, however, the regular Mississippi delegates and their Southern supporters pointed to the lack of any national standards by which the delegate-selection process could be judged—in Mississippi or anywhere else. They argued that to seat the challengers solely on the basis of discrimination they allegedly had suffered in the past would be arbitrary, unfair, and without precedent in Democratic Party history.

On direct orders from President Johnson, a negotiating team led by Senator Hubert Humphrey and UAW President Walter Reuther began seeking some form of compromise that,

above all else, would hold the convention together. Under
the compromise they finally drafted, the Mississippi regulars were required to sign a stringent loyalty oath; the Mississippi Freedom Democratic Party challengers were awarded
two at-large delegate seats; language was adopted for inclu-
sion in the Call to the 1968 Democratic National Convention
guaranteeing "that voters in the States(s), regardless of race,
color, creed or national origin, will have the opportunity to
participate fully in Party affairs"; and a Special Equal Rights
Committee of the Democratic National Committee was created to assist the states in meeting these new requirements.

Both contending parties—the regulars and the loyalists from
Mississippi—rejected the compromise. But the convention
adopted it enthusiastically and the feared Southern exodus
was averted. Of longer-term significance, the basis now existed
for the national party at future conventions to reject any
delegation selected by discriminatory or exclusionary procedures.

Two points should be underscored. First, the focus in 1964
was to remedy racial discrimination in the delegate-selection
process, not the exclusion of rank-and-file Democrats generally.
Second, the Atlantic City compromise, although it brought
the national party directly into the delegate-selection process
for the first time, was fundamentally an extension of the
process of gradual adjustment and accommodation at earlier
conventions in dealing with the civil rights issue. The preservation of a united party that could go into the general
election at maximum strength remained the principal motivation in reaching the compromise. The goal of opening the
party nominating processes to broad-scale grassroots participation was to await the arrival of the Vietnam War as the
Democrats' most divisive issue.

ADVENT OF ACTIVISM

By the fall of 1967, it was certain that the presidential nominating process of the Democratic Party would play a critical
role in the plans of the antiwar activists, Democratic and

otherwise. Their strategy called for a national mobilization of grassroots workers, primarily students, to support the candidacy of Senator Eugene McCarthy, who, after initially refusing to run, finally agreed to challenge the incumbent President for the nomination as the most realistic way of forcing some change in his policies of military escalation. Following McCarthy's encouraging showing in New Hampshire (he still lost to a Johnson write-in campaign) and Senator Robert Kennedy's decision to announce his candidacy, the Democratic Party was faced with the most serious challenge to its established leadership in this century. The President's decision, announced on March 31, 1968, not to seek renomination only intensified the efforts of the antiwar activists to transform the Democratic Party into their principal instrument for ending the war.

The importance of this development cannot be overstressed. Traditionally, the presidential nominating process is a pragmatic testing of the relative political appeals and strengths of the contending candidates, all of whom share the ultimate goal of winning the Presidency in the general election. Although the struggle is often bitter and hard-fought, the contenders are prepared generally to accept the process as it is and to develop their political strategies accordingly. All the contenders recognize that, in the end, they cannot afford the total estrangement of their opponents if the eventual winner of the nomination is to have a reasonable chance of winning the general election.

For a substantial number of people who participated in the Democratic delegate-selection process in 1968, this traditional purpose and the traditional assumptions were superseded by the far more critical objective, in their view, of capturing the Democratic Party as the first step in reversing U.S. policy in Indochina. Governor Harold E. Hughes of Iowa, later a U.S. senator, put it directly in his speech at the convention nominating Eugene McCarthy for President: "Vietnam is by no means the only issue. But it is the key issue; the symbolic issue." [3] This conception changed the whole character of the nominating struggle, bringing it much closer to a moral crusade, a contest between the forces of good and evil.

In these circumstances, thousands of grassroots supporters of the antiwar candidates—McCarthy, Kennedy, and Mc-Govern—came into the primaries and the various party meetings in the states where delegates were selected by county and state conventions. Being new to the Democratic Party, or in many instances new to political activity of any kind, they had little stake in preserving the party structure and procedures as they found them and everything to gain by changing the rules in a manner that would enhance their power. These inclinations grew more intense as the newcomers encountered practices in many states that effectively frustrated their plans for capturing state delegations and building the antiwar coalition.

These events coincided with the implementation of the non-discrimination standards that had been approved by the 1964 National Convention. In July 1967, Governor Richard J. Hughes of New Jersey, chairman of the Special Equal Rights Committee, wrote to all Democratic state chairmen and Democratic National Committee members advising them of the six criteria that would have to be observed in selecting delegates to the 1968 convention. Failure to observe the "six basic elements," as they came to be known, would seriously jeopardize any delegation's seats in the event of a credentials challenge based on racial discrimination or exclusion.

Although the standards were drafted to halt racial discrimination in the delegate-selection process, it was only a short step for the procedural guarantees to be extended to the delegate-selection process generally. In other years, there would have been less motivation to develop this broader application; in 1968, however, the antiwar candidacies of McCarthy, Kennedy, and McGovern provided the motive force eventually to challenge the entire nominating structure—primaries, state conventions, party caucuses, and the national convention itself. This coincidence of opportunity and motivation would affect the future of the Democratic Party in ways unimagined by the architects of the 1964 compromise.

The public's attention was, as usual, directed to the primary election battle where McCarthy and Kennedy were dividing the antiwar vote. But in 1968, as before, a majority of the delegates (59.3 per cent) would be selected in state conventions and by party caucuses, institutions better insulated from popular pressures, and by procedures that favored party leaders of established authority and influence. In the main, these leaders opposed the antiwar challenge of McCarthy and Kennedy and, not surprisingly, responded to the appeals of Vice President Humphrey. To oversimplify: While McCarthy and Kennedy battled for delegate votes in the primaries, Humphrey scored impressive victories in the state conventions and party caucuses. His first-ballot victory was never seriously in doubt, at least in the weeks after Robert Kennedy's assassination.

As thousands of new Democratic activists gathered in Chicago in late August, they sensed that, although they could stop a sitting President from seeking renomination, they were essentially powerless to stop the selection of his Vice President as the party's nominee for President. The anger and violence that erupted inside the International Amphitheatre and outside the Conrad Hilton were the predictable response of people who had embarked on a great moral crusade only to be deprived of their ultimate triumph by procedures and traditions that, in their opinion, were patently unfair and unacceptable.

Their outrage was given a substantive focus by the *ad hoc* Commission on the Democratic Selection of Presidential Nominees, headed by Governor Harold Hughes, which had been asked by the 1968 Credentials Committee and the Committee on Rules and the Order of Business to initiate an investigation of the procedures used in selecting delegates to the Chicago convention. "We have concluded," Hughes's commission said, "that state systems for selecting delegates to the National Convention and the procedures of the Convention itself, display considerably less fidelity to basic democratic principles than a nation which claims to govern itself can safely tolerate." The commission then listed a number of specific reforms that became the basis for the delegate-selection guidelines adopted by the Democratic National Committee in 1971.[4]

The activists in Chicago lost their battle to nominate an antiwar candidate and to write an antiwar platform. But, almost unnoticed at the time, they achieved two victories that irreversibly changed the posture of the national Democratic Party toward internal reform.

First, the national convention adopted a resolution from the Credentials Committee and the minority report from the Rules Committee that legitimized the extension of the procedural guarantees against racial discrimination in delegate selection to all aspects of the nominating process, including the conduct of the convention itself, and created two special commissions to define specifically and implement this broadened mandate. In the words of the majority report of the Credentials Committee, adopted by the convention on August 28, 1968: "We can and should encourage appropriate revisions in the delegate selection process to assure the fullest possible participation and to make the Democratic Party completely representative of grass roots sentiment."

Second, the bitter struggle over the nomination, in the states and at the national convention, exposed procedures and practices so indefensible that the burden of proof within the party shifted to those opposing delegate-selection and convention reforms and away from those who advocated these actions. This shift of sentiment, especially among the Washington-based leaders who would preside over national party affairs, elevated the matter of internal reform to a priority position that it steadfastly maintained through the 1972 convention.

POLITICS OF REFORM

The struggle within the Democratic Party over the Vietnam War lifted the issue of party reform to a new plateau of activity and commitment. Unlike 1964, when the scope of the proposed reforms was restricted to what was needed to preserve a fragile unity within the party, the post-1968 objective of democratizing internal party procedures became, for many persons, an all-consuming end in itself. Such an environment was not conducive, to say the least, to the kind of pragmatic compromises and more gradual accommodations that had worked in the past.

There did emerge, however, a rationale for the reform effort that stressed the long-term political benefits that supposedly would accrue to the country and the Democratic Party if it remained faithful to the reform mandate. This theme runs through all the basic speeches of the reform advocates and the principal reform documents. *Mandate for Reform*, the report of the Commission on Party Structure and Delegate Selection, closed with these words:

> We believe that popular participation is more than a proud heritage of our party, more than a first principle. We believe that popular control of the Democratic Party is necessary for its survival. . . . If we are not an open party; if we do not represent the demands of change, then the danger is not that people will go to the Republican Party; it is that there will no longer be a way for people committed to orderly change to fulfill their needs and desires within our traditional political system. It is that they will turn to third and fourth party politics or the anti-politics of the street.[5]

Fred Dutton, an ideologist of the New Politics and a member of the McGovern-Fraser Commission, emphasized the new sources of political power that were available to a political party with the imagination to attract them. In his *Changing Sources of Power*, Dutton said:

> The large number of new voters and the high level of independence among them reinforce the probability that a critical passage in the politics of this country is at hand. . . . A clear-cut coalescing within this large sector even close to that of the New Deal generation could give it a significant measure of political power not only for the 1970s but well beyond. It is only a coincidence that this group will be moving into the electorate just as the New Deal generation's ranks are thinning and its public influence is slackening . . . there could be a quite literal passing of the political torch from one cornerstone generation to another.[6]

Democratic National Chairman O'Brien expressed this view in his year-end report for 1971. He said:

> If significant numbers of young people, women, minorities, and others alienated by traditional political institutions are actively involved in the nominating process, a revitalized and recharged Democratic Party almost surely will emerge in the general election campaign. I have no doubt that these votes—when combined with more traditional sources of Democratic strength—could spell the difference between victory and defeat in November 1972.

A number of assumptions—largely unstated and unquestioned— were buried beneath these assertions. It was assumed, for example, that millions of Americans, dissatisfied and unhappy in their daily lives, distrustful of their political leaders, were eagerly awaiting only the chance to recapture, as it was usually said, "control over their own destinies" through direct political action. More specifically, it was assumed that the 25 million first-time voters in 1972 would jump at the opportunity to begin remaking the society and the political system that repelled so many of them. Finally, it was assumed that the new grassroots Democrats attracted by the reality of an open party could simply be grafted to the established Democratic coalition, thereby assuring the party's majority position for the foreseeable future.

These assumptions were open to question. As was noted in the last chapter, the political chemistry of alienation, for many persons, did not always respond to McGovern's advocacy of reform. Not only did a majority of those who believed the system was rigged in favor of the special interests prefer Nixon over McGovern, but they also held relatively hard-line views on issues such as race and permissiveness that were offended by McGovern's brand of populism.

These assumptions were fed, no doubt, by many poll findings. In May 1968, for example, the Gallup Poll found that 33 percent of the public (and 41 percent of those under thirty years of age) said they would be "willing to work as a volunteer" for their political party in the coming campaign. Gallup later reported that 14 per cent of college students surveyed said they had worked for a political organization in the 1970 congressional elections: 8 per cent for the Democratic Party, 4 per cent for the Republicans and 2 per cent for other parties. As the 1972 elections approached, it appeared that a vast army of volunteers could be mobilized if even a tiny fraction of the 15 per cent of McGovern's backers nationwide who said they planned to "work for a party or a candidate in this election" actually followed through.

In the primaries, McGovern recruited an impressive force of volunteers, particularly in California. After Miami Beach, however, antagonisms between McGovern's lieutenants (both in Washington and in the states) and local political leaders frequently reduced the impact of the volunteer army that re-enlisted for the general election. Of most importance, McGovern's lack of credibility as a President created a barrier that no amount of organizational expertise could surmount.

Beyond McGovern's organizational problems was the mistaken assumption that an overwhelming majority of the new voters in 1972 would automatically respond to McGovern's brand of the New Politics. A special analysis by the Gallup Poll in July 1972 (see Table 6) revealed that Nixon, not McGovern, held the advantage with unregistered persons between eighteen and twenty-four years of age. Although McGovern was favored among registered voters under twenty-four years, Nixon was preferred by those who had not yet registered.[7]

TABLE 6

| | Percentage Favoring: | | |
	Nixon	McGovern	Undecided
Registered	41	57	2
Unregistered	46	43	11

And even among the college students, presumed to be the vanguard of the New Politics, the trend was *against* McGovern as the campaign wore on. In the spring of 1972, the Gallup Poll found college students dividing 61–35 per cent in favor of McGovern, with 4 per cent undecided. By early October, however, the split had narrowed to 49–47 per cent in favor of the senator, with 4 per cent undecided.

It is revealing that the only persons to question any of these assumptions during the McGovern-Fraser Commission's debate over the new delegate-selection guidelines were state Democratic chairmen, such as Will Davis of Texas and George Mitchell of Maine, men who had personally experienced the difficult problems of organizing and maintaining an effective party on the state level.

If the rationale supporting reform had not prevailed so totally in the post-1968 period, at least among those Democrats with the responsibility for carrying out the convention's mandates, it might have been possible to approach the assignment with a more discerning eye to the critical organizational problems that inevitably were part of the reform equation. And this kind of hard questioning and probing, in turn, might have produced a more balanced effort that sought, on the one hand, to remedy the admitted inequities in the process without, on the other hand, sacrificing the valuable perspective and experience of established Democratic leaders, particularly on the state level. As it turned out, however, it took a brave and resilient Democrat to suggest that the party's reform effort did not represent the most propitious combination of Jacksonian democracy and political opportunity to come along since the early days of the New Deal.

WORK OF THE REFORM COMMISSIONS

Senator Fred Harris, then Democratic National Chairman, appointed the two reform commissions in early 1969. He selected Senator George McGovern of South Dakota as chairman of the Commission on Party Structure and Delegate Selection and Senator Harold Hughes of Iowa as vice chairman—a pecking order that left Senator Hughes somewhat disgruntled since his *ad hoc* commission had provided most of the documentation and the impetus for the expanded reform commitment voted by the Chicago convention. Representative James G. O'Hara of Michigan was named chairman of the Commission on Rules. Although it could be said, and it frequently was, that all segments of the party were represented on the commissions, the larger truth suggested that those persons favoring a vigorous and sweeping reform effort were in the majority. It is also true that the activist reformers came to all the meetings of the commission and were always agreed on their objectives in advance. Organized labor, represented on the commission by I. W. Abel of the Steelworkers, simply boycotted the entire affair by totally abstaining from the commission's work. The more moderate members were spotty in their attendance. The significance of attendance is illustrated by the fact that the most controversial of the guidelines, A-1 and A-2, which resulted in *de facto* quotas, were adopted by a vote of 10–9, with nine members absent.

After some initial disagreements over the scope of the respective mandates of the two commissions, it was agreed that the McGovern Commission (later termed the McGovern-Fraser Commission when Representative Don Fraser of Minnesota assumed the chairmanship following McGovern's resignation to seek the presidential nomination) would focus on the process by which state parties selected national convention delegates and the O'Hara Commission would deal with the organization and conduct of the national convention, plus the related question of the convention's size and the apportionment of delegates among the states. Both commissions hired small professional staffs, supplemented by numbers of academic advisers, college interns, and volunteers.

The early months, in part, were devoted to exhaustive research efforts to discover the facts: how the states and territories actually selected their convention delegates and the rules and procedures under which the national convention actually functioned. In both instances, the research produced a factual base that was unique; never before in the party's history had this information been brought together in one place in an orderly manner.

Simultaneously with the research, public hearings in Washington and sixteen other cities were held to solicit the opinions of all persons who had something to say. Drafts of proposed guidelines, rules, issues, alternatives, and the like were extensively circulated among interested Democrats and others for their comments. Both commissions held numerous meetings as the members thrashed out the complicated problems that came to light. Even the most severe critics of the reforms recognize the commission's extraordinary expenditure of time, energy, and—for Democrats the most precious commodity of all—money. It is hard to recall comparable examples of volunteer national party groups that worked as diligently.

DELEGATE-SELECTION REFORM

The McGovern-Fraser Commission had the job of defining in specific language how the state parties would implement the convention's mandate to give "all Democratic voters . . . a full, meaningful, and timely opportunity to participate" in the delegate-selection process. A number of changes were readily apparent and relatively noncontroversial. For example, every state party was required to adopt and make easily available written party rules that encouraged maximum participation among interested Democrats; proxy voting was forbidden; a quorum of 40 per cent was required for all party committees involved in delegate selection; the unit rule was forbidden at all stages of delegate selection (a change initially voted by the 1968 convention); adequate public notice of all meetings was required; and all delegates had to be chosen in the calendar year of the convention.

Other reforms were more controversial: State parties were prohibited from choosing more than 10 per cent of the delegation by party committees—the process most removed from popular participation; in states where slates of potential delegates were assembled, the same procedural safeguards were required in the slatemaking process; no public or party officeholders could be appointed as delegates by virtue of their official position; and in states using the convention system, at least 75 per cent of the delegates had to be chosen at the congressional district or smaller unit levels.[8]

The thrust of these reforms was consistent and fully defensible in light of the convention's reform resolutions. *Mandate for Reform* stated it well:

The guidelines that we have adopted are designed to open the door to all Democrats who seek a voice in their Party's most important decision: the choice of its presidential nominee. We are concerned with the opportunity to participate, rather than the actual level of participation . . . we are less concerned with the product of the meetings than the process, although we believe that the product will be improved in the give and take of open and fairly conducted meetings.[9]

If these sentiments had, in fact, been reflected in the McGovern Commission's final product—or if other Democratic leaders had demanded the faithful application of these standards—much of the unhappiness ensuing from eighteen guidelines, not to mention the damage to the party itself, might have been avoided. But the reform of the delegate-selection process got into trouble precisely at the point where certain of the commission members, in an excess of zeal to accomplish their goal of opening the party, created conditions that encouraged the same kind of procedural irregularities that the guidelines were supposed to abolish and, as an extra dividend, contributed to the flight of Democratic professionals as active participants in the nominating process.

To be more precise, guidelines A-1 and A-2 required, in effect, that state parties and, at a later date, the presidential contenders prove their fidelity to openness and popular participation by the presence of minority groups, women, and young people on their delegations "in reasonable relationship to the groups' presence in the population of the state." The commission went on to say, in a footnote, that "this is not to be accomplished by the mandatory imposition of quotas," thereby creating an insoluble dilemma that was never satisfactorily resolved.[10] No other guidelines loomed larger than these for the state parties as they began to make the extensive changes in their delegate-selection procedures. (Not a single state party had rules or procedures that initially qualified under the eighteen guidelines.) How, in an open and democratic process, could a specific predetermined result—a certain proportion of blacks, women, and youth delegates—be achieved without impinging upon the very open and democratic pro-

cedures that were now required by the national party? Every
time this question was raised, and it was asked repeatedly by
state party leaders, the commission's answer was the same:
There is *no* quota system, the guidelines make that clear. But
there *are* affirmative-action goals that you must strive to meet
in selecting your state's delegation. The 1972 Credentials Committee, and ultimately the convention itself, will be the final
judge of whether or not your state took the necessary steps to
overcome the effects of past discrimination against these three
groups within the party.

This, of course, was really no answer at all, in the sense of
giving state party leaders any exact notion of what would be
expected of them when their delegations arrived at the convention. In an effort to reduce the uncertainties, the commission
staff prepared a list of suggested affirmative actions that states
could follow to involve greater numbers of blacks, women,
and young people. On November 29, 1971, Chairman Fraser
issued this further clarification:

> We believe that state parties should be on notice that whenever
> the proportion of women, minorities, and young people in a
> delegation offered for seating in Miami is less than the proportion
> of these groups in the total population, and the delegation is
> challenged on the grounds that Guidelines A-1 and A-2 were not
> complied with, such a challenge will constitute a *prima facie*
> showing of violation of the Guidelines, and the Democratic Party
> along with the challenged delegation has the burden of showing
> that the state party took full and affirmative action to achieve
> such representation, including an *effective* affirmative action pro-
> gram along the lines outlined in our policy statement adopted in
> October, 1971.

Democratic National Chairman O'Brien added a covering
note to the state chairman emphasizing the importance of
Fraser's declaration.

Although it was not the meaning intended by Fraser, many
state chairmen concluded that assuming the burden of proof
of *effective* affirmative action, in the politically charged en-

vironment of the convention's Credentials Committee, was tantamount to being found guilty. After all, an *effective* program would seem to be one that worked. And the fact of a credentials challenge—in itself—would seem to suggest the ineffectiveness of the state party's effort. The Fraser letter was a significant step toward establishing a *de facto* quota system, regardless of denials continuing to issue from the commission.

Other developments increased the pressure on state parties to make sure that the "reasonable relationship" was guaranteed between a group's presence in the state's population and its presence on the delegation. Meetings of O'Brien and Fraser with delegations representing the Black Caucus, the Women's Political Caucus, and the National Youth Caucus produced ringing declarations that the A-1 and A-2 guidelines would be enforced, come what may, and that any significant departure from the appropriate numbers would be interpreted as *prima facie* evidence of noncompliance.

In the early primaries and state conventions, it was clear that one candidate in particular—George McGovern—was taking special pains to see that his delegates were in strict compliance with the "reasonable relationship" criterion. As a matter of fact, McGovern frequently had extra blacks, women, and young people, to make sure the message got through. His opponents for the nomination could only assume, and they did, that their delegates would be challenged by the McGovern forces on the basis of A-1 and A-2, even if all other standards of delegate selection had been rigidly followed. Thus his opponents began adding and subtracting individuals in states where their delegations appeared to be vulnerable by insufficient representation of women, minorities, or young people.

Take Hubert Humphrey's efforts to increase the percentage of women on his Pennsylvania delegation, for example. Despite a concerted effort to recruit women to run as Humphrey delegates in the April 25 primary, the election produced a Humphrey delegation in which women comprised only 36 per cent, a number very likely to produce a challenge from the Women's Political Caucus or from other candidates.

Twenty-five per cent of the total Pennsylvania delegation, however, remained to be chosen by the delegates already elected and by the state Democratic committee. Humphrey fired off a strong letter to his supporters urging them, in effect, to fill almost all of his remaining vacancies with women, thereby bringing his total percentage of women at least to the 40 per cent mark. But this action, in turn, produced loud outcries from the state labor union officials who had strongly backed Humphrey in the primary and who had been counting on many of these positions for themselves. About half of the remaining vacancies were filled with women, averting some, but not all, of the challenges. In the end, the Credentials Committee arrived at a compromise that added eighteen women with a half vote each to the Pennsylvania delegation and reduced eighteen men to a comparable half-vote status.

The considerable attention in the press and on television to these efforts to expand representation of women, minorities, and young people helped build the impression that this aspect of the delegate-selection process was critical in the struggle for the presidential nomination. This, however, was not the case; all the contenders, not just McGovern, had their women, their minorities, and their young people contending for delegate seats. It was probably easier for McGovern to recruit women and young people, but the others—Muskie and Humphrey, in particular—quickly recognized the wisdom of meeting the general requirements of the A-1 and A-2 guidelines and did so.

Whatever benefit McGovern acquired from the new rules resulted from the less-publicized changes that greatly reduced the control of established party leaders in selecting delegates or in influencing their selection. The practice of choosing delegates by state party committees was almost totally eliminated; the appointment of delegates by virtue of their party or public office was totally banned. And no delegate could be selected prior to January 1, 1972.

The impact of these changes was especially evident in non-primary states. Precinct leaders who would routinely meet with a known group of friends and neighbors to choose delegates for county or state conventions suddenly encountered a mass outpouring of new people who arrived early, stayed late, and, more often than not, supported George McGovern. In many ways, it was a reversal of 1968: Hubert Humphrey was forced to stake his candidacy on his showing in the primaries, while George McGovern was cleaning up in the convention states.

CREDENTIALS CONTESTS

Despite widespread implementation of the reforms, the 1972 Credentials Committee still had to resolve eighty-two challenges in thirty-one state delegations. Twenty-one of the states faced challenges that related to the composition of delegations under A-1 and A-2. Many of those challenges were initiated by the Women's Political Caucus or the National Youth Caucus in the interests of women and young people. But in a large number of cases this had the operational effect of challenging non-McGovern delegates with persons who—if seated—intended to vote for McGovern. It soon became clear that most of the challenges, in result if not in initial motivation, were distinctly candidate-oriented—an effort by one presidential contender to win additional delegates on the basis of alleged violations in the selection of his opponents' delegates. The reforms, in other words, became an offensive weapon in the battle for the nomination, as distinguished from an effort simply to democratize and open the Democratic Party to grassroots sentiment. That this development was fully predictable made it no less a departure from the wording and spirit of the recommendations of the McGovern-Fraser Commission.[11]

This intense *candidate*, as opposed to *party*, orientation carried over into the deliberations and decisions of the Credentials Committee and, subsequently, to the floor of the national convention. The Commission on Rules had designed what essentially was a judicial model for the settlement of credentials disputes, stressing the building of a factual record

and the guarantees of procedural due process for the contending parties. This model was uniquely ill suited to a situation
where decisions would be made, in large part, on whether
they enhanced or reduced a candidate's delegate count.

As a consequence, the Credentials Committee evolved a
procedure that looked to informal negotiations among the
contending parties as the most realistic way of settling most
of the disputes. Challenged delegates were certified, replaced,
or, in many cases, reduced to half-vote status in conjunction
with the addition of half-vote delegates from among the challengers on the basis of voting strength that the contending
parties could muster among the Credentials Committee members. Deals were cut, compromises designed, and alliances
established in very much the traditional manner. The ABM
(Anybody But McGovern) alliance that initially defeated the
McGovern forces on the California challenge, for example,
arose out of a common desire among the other contenders to
block his nomination and out of a shared sense of frustration
and outrage over the seemingly endless challenges over the
numbers of women and young people on their delegations.

It is beyond the scope of this book to recount the details of
the credentials battles that unfolded before network television
cameras at the Credentials Committee meetings in mid-June
and subsequently on the floor of the national convention.
But it is clearly our responsibility to ask this question: How
did this final step in the reform process look to the nation at
large and, especially, to the millions of viewers who considered
themselves Democrats?

The evidence is conflicting and seemingly contradictory. On
the one hand, the Harris Survey reported surprising levels
of public support for the Democratic Party's efforts to open its
doors and to bring new groups into the nominating process.
Harris told the National Press Club three days after the
presidential election that

> . . . majorities of 70–19 per cent liked seeing greater representation
> for young people, by 81–13 per cent liked giving women more
> delegate seats, by 76–17 per cent liked giving blacks and the

Spanish-speaking a greater role, and agreed, 73–19 per cent, that the Democratic Convention was more "open than any before." [12]

These data would appear to illustrate the positive side of a growing public unhappiness with institutions that appear unwilling or unable to respond affirmatively to popular pressures for greater access and influence at the individual level. No one who witnessed the Democratic Party's credentials disputes could doubt the reality of change in the composition of delegations that collectively represented the national Democratic Party. Its capacity to change old traditions and procedures in order to achieve greater responsiveness to a segment of the Democratic rank-and-file should be counted as a solid achievement, and according to Harris it was so recognized by the public.

On the other hand, it is impossible to dismiss reports from Democratic leaders in all sections of the country of a strong negative reaction to the apparent imposition of quotas in determining the composition of some delegations. The notion of a person's sex, age, or race as the determining factor in winning delegate status collided with the deep-seated, conventional belief that a person should make it on his or her own in free and open competition. The Illinois challenge—in which popularly elected delegates were unseated in favor of a carefully balanced slate of challengers—was the most dramatic example of what appeared to be the outright perversion of the democratic process in the name of party reform.

Without question, the goal of opening the nominating process to new groups and new faces stimulated a generally favorable public reaction. But the achievement of this goal produced considerable disaffection among party leaders and allied interest groups, especially segments of organized labor, on whom the Democrats traditionally relied in the general election campaign. And, to the extent that some of these new faces appeared through the operations of a *de facto* quota system instead of through the open competition that the reforms were instituted to achieve, this positive public reaction was diluted. This was especially true among the more traditional "casual Democrats," [13] who encountered on television a greatly changed, if not unattractive, Democratic Party gathered in Convention Hall at Miami Beach.

CONVENTION REFORM

The work of the Commission on Rules was carried off with less controversy and less impact on the party itself, except as the party exists in the period of the national convention. But this fact does not blunt the basic conclusion about the commission's work: The largest national nominating convention in American history, with a daily agenda filled to overflowing with controversial items, functioned in an orderly and sensible, if lengthy, manner—in stark contrast to the chaos and disorder that had prevailed in Chicago four years earlier.

The commission's most controversial duty concerned the apportionment among the states of the 3,000 delegates to the national convention. From the outset, it was obvious that the populous industrial states—the base of Democratic strength in the general election—were grievously underrepresented on the basis of past apportionment formulae. To remedy these inequities, the Commission on Rules recommended to the Democratic National Committee a formula that allocated half of the delegates among the states in accordance with each state's population in the 1970 census, the other half to be allocated among the states in direct ratio to each state's Democratic presidential vote in the last three elections—1960, 1964, and 1968. States such as New York, Pennsylvania, California, Michigan, New Jersey, and Illinois stood to gain a significant number of delegates at the expense of smaller and Southern states. (For example, New York's delegation would increase from 190 out of 2,622 in 1968 to 301 out of 3,000; Tennessee's would drop from 51 out of 2,622 to 49 out of 3,000.) [14]

After hours of heated debate, the Democratic National Committee on February 19, 1971—the same meeting that unanimously adopted the delegate-selection guidelines as part of the 1972 Call—modified the Commission on Rules' recommended formula. Electoral College strength was substituted for raw population in the allocation of 53 per cent of the delegates, and the commission's proposal for using the presidential vote of the past three elections was retained as the basis for distributing the remaining 47 per cent of the delegates. The change caused a small increase in the number of delegates for the less populous states and was not quite as harsh on Southern states that had voted Republican or American Independent in the last three presidential elections. A group of reform Democrats filed suit in the federal courts challenging the constitutionality of the amended formula, but the courts eventually upheld the National Committee's decision.

Apart from the apportionment formula, the burden of the Rules Commission's work dealt with designing fair and sensible procedures for all aspects of the convention's work toward the goal of making the convention "representative, open, deliberative, and fair." [15] Some of the proposals reformed the planning and management of the convention: an elected, instead of an appointed, convention manager; an elected arrangements committee that included nonvoting representatives of all presidential candidates; the designation of hotel accommodations by lot; and the installation of extensive communications equipment available to all convention participants.

Other recommendations dealt with the operations of the convention's committees: specific administrative procedures for filing and deciding credentials challenges; regional public hearings by the platform committee; proportional voting strength among the states on the major convention committees; and the printing of the major committee reports ten days in advance of the convention to facilitate greater understanding of the proposals among the delegates and the general public.

Finally, the commission made a number of recommendations dealing with the conduct of the convention itself: a set of written convention rules (for the first time in Democratic Party history); abolition of the motion to table, so that delegates would have to vote on the substance of issues; a ban on

motions offered from the floor (except under suspension of
the rules that required a two-thirds vote), so that the delegates
would not be forced to vote on unexpected and often poorly
understood motions; floor seating of delegations and the roll
of the states determined by lot; the elimination of favorite-son
nominations; a strict time limit on nominating and seconding
speeches; and the elimination of staged floor demonstrations.

Despite the length of the convention sessions and the controversial nature of many issues that came to the floor for
final disposition, the delegates generally knew what was going
on and why. They stayed in their seats—right through the
night on two occasions—and maintained the deliberative
character of this 3,000-plus delegate assembly. To be sure, the
delegates didn't always agree with everything that happened,
but the charges of unfairness and arbitrary action were at a
minimum.[16]

WHAT WENT WRONG?

What, then, is one to make of this unique effort to change
the rules, procedures, and behavioral patterns of the oldest
political party among Western democracies? How, indeed,
could the Democrats do so many of the "right" things and
end up so poorly on Election Day?

Part of the answer, of course—one that we have already explored in the previous chapter—is that the Nixon landslide
was partially a creation of George McGovern, and it would be
unfair, not to mention wrong, to blame delegate-selection
and convention reforms for his disastrous presidential campaign. But, for several reasons, this cannot be the whole
answer.

The ideology and rhetoric of party reform—the stirring
declarations about participatory democracy and giving the
people a greater voice in their own destiny—masked a much
more traditional and basic struggle: Who runs the Democratic
Party? One need not belittle George McGovern's commitment to opening the Democratic Party to greater rank-and-
file involvement by pointing out that a large number of the

new Democrats who took advantage of the reforms were enthusiastic McGovern supporters. McGovern's success in helping establish delegate-selection reform as the priority concern of the national party—apart from his considerable skill in using the reformed rules and procedures to advantage in the actual competition for delegates—stands as a political achievement of considerable dimension. George McGovern was not handed the Democratic Party's presidential nomination on a silver platter; he won it in the primaries and state conventions by amassing more votes than his competitors. Although it has been learned subsequently that the Nixon forces did their best to disrupt the primary campaigns of McGovern's principal rivals—Muskie, Humphrey, and Jackson—there is no evidence that these activities, however outrageous, had a decisive effect on the eventual outcome of the nominating process.

But McGovern's considerable achievement could not negate the reality that the Democratic Party, in 1972, found itself in a frustrating dilemma of legitimacy, one that must be resolved before 1976 if winning the Presidency is to be a realistic goal. Those Democrats who had felt themselves most abused by the nominating process in 1968 looked to the success of the delegate-selection reforms as the only way the party could earn their loyalty in 1972. In this sense, the full implementation of the reforms, including criteria of the A-1 and A-2 guidelines, became the party's principal weapon in forestalling the mass defection of antiwar activists, New Politicians, and others generally dismayed by the traditional nominating procedures.

But a price was paid for that success. The gradual evolution of a strong desire to open the party to women, minorities, and young people via a *de facto* quota system that guaranteed their presence, in combination with the elimination of the traditional procedures by which most elected Democratic leaders became delegates, resulted in the serious underrepresentation of another important constituency, the "casual Democrats"—the nonactivists who rarely attend precinct caucuses or state conventions and often don't even vote in primaries. But these are also the people who, on Election Day, usually can be counted on to vote Democratic, and these are the Democrats George McGovern lost by the millions—because they either voted for Richard Nixon or just stayed home.

Democrats who hold elective office—public or party—traditionally speak for these casual Democrats. They are best equipped to sense their moods and attitudes since they comprise a significant portion of most Democratic constituencies. The early and unexpected collapse of the Muskie candidacy left a number of prominent governors, senators, House members, and party leaders embarrassed, politically exposed, and gun-shy. But the restrictions on the *ex officio* designation of delegates meant that these Democratic leaders had to compete actively for a delegate's seat at Miami Beach. In these circumstances, a large number of Democratic leaders who otherwise might have exerted considerable influence on the contest for the nomination and in writing the platform simply stepped to the sidelines rather than compete for delegate status with a new and unpredictable collection of political activists, many of whom possessed the seeming advantage of being female or black or under thirty-one years of age.

This withdrawal of elected Democratic leadership from the nominating process left a void that was never filled at the national convention and contributed to a void that persisted throughout the presidential campaign itself. It is not just coincidence that the flight of Democratic politicians from Miami Beach and the presidential campaign occurred in a year when certain of the delegate-selection reforms made their involvement less than easy and, in some cases, nearly impossible.

The Democratic Party, in other words, fought the battle of legitimacy in its reform effort and achieved a legitimate result in terms of the rules laid down by the two reform commissions. But this same effort acquired a distinctly illegitimate flavor for many casual Democrats—an essential element of a winning presidential coalition—through the operation of what they perceived as *de facto* quotas and the peculiar absence of Democratic leaders who traditionally have been their spokesmen and advocates.

The diminished role of elected Democrats in the 1972 nominating process had one additional grave consequence: It reinforced the intense candidate orientation of the participants and lessened the concern that was exhibited for the party itself. To put it bluntly, a proportion of George McGovern's most enthusiastic supporters would have severed all Democratic ties if their man had failed to win. The candidate, in the final preconvention weeks, did little to discourage this attitude. He said in a *Life* magazine interview:

> . . . if a bunch of old established politicians gang up to prevent me from getting the nomination, because I didn't come to them for help . . . then I will not let them get away with it. There's been so much hard work and emotion poured into this campaign by so many thousands of people—it would be such an infuriating, disillusioning experience for them all—that I would repudiate the whole process. I would run as an independent or support somebody else on an independent ticket.[17]

As we have seen, the reforms from the outset were justified primarily as a way to preserve not only the Democratic Party but the two-party system. And yet, in the closing week before Miami Beach, the party was almost forgotten in the bitter struggle between the McGovern and Humphrey forces. It even appeared at times that many of McGovern's most ardent supporters—if not McGovern himself—saw winning the nomination, and not the subsequent run for the Presidency, as their principal objective. Having been turned away and defeated at Chicago, the new generation of Democrats who came to Miami Beach wanted to win, to nominate their man and write their platform, largely as vindication of their earlier, unsuccessful effort. Where the Democratic Party fitted into these designs was never totally clear.

Because important elements of the year-round Democratic Party were nonparticipants in the nominating process, it is not surprising that these same elements exhibited a minimum interest in the presidential campaign during the postconvention period. The same cry could be heard in all sections of the country: "The McGovern people were good enough to win the nomination, they ought to be good enough to run the campaign without my help." As a result, George McGovern waged one of the most lonely—and most courageous—campaigns in memory.

This chapter is not intended to argue, in any sense, for a return to the nominating system that existed prior to 1972. The positive image of the Democratic Party as open and responsive to popular involvement, clearly detected by pollster Louis Harris, should be seen as an extremely valuable asset to be used in 1976 and subsequent presidential years. But it does suggest that wisdom lies in recapturing some of the pragmatic common sense that characterized the earlier reforms adopted at Atlantic City in 1964, which frankly recognized unacceptable practices and proposed a remedy that (a) laid the foundation for future progress and (b) stopped short of sacrificing the broad support of party leaders and workers needed in the general election. It does suggest that reforms, to be workable, cannot become an end in themselves but must remain one element in the much broader effort to win the Presidency. This means developing procedures more likely to produce an outcome that is viewed as legitimate not only by highly motivated activists—the people ready to take full advantage of an open nominating process—but also by the segment of the party that comprehends, and communicates with, the millions of casual Democrats without whose support victory in the general election is impossible.

3

DEMOCRATS
WHO WEREN'T
SUPPOSED
TO WIN BUT DID

The problems of the Democratic Party as manifested in George McGovern's campaign for the Presidency are serious and deep-rooted. But the fact of their existence is at least balanced if not outweighed by another compelling fact: The erosion of party loyalty so evident at the presidential level in most instances has not seeped downward to erode the appeal of Democratic candidates at the state and local level.

This was true in 1968, when the Democrats retained control of Congress despite Richard Nixon's narrow victory over Hubert Humphrey, making Nixon the first President since Zachary Taylor in 1848 to win a first term in the White House without a majority of his own party in the Congress. As we have seen, it was true again in 1970, when the Democrats withstood a highly organized and well-financed attempt by the GOP to capture the U.S. Senate and, to the surprise of many political experts, not to mention Democrats, scored impressively in the gubernatorial races.

And it was true again in 1972, as the Democrats made a net gain of two Senate seats, held the GOP to a pick-up of twelve seats in the House (where they needed a net gain of thirty-nine for a majority), and increased their majority of governorships by one (thirty-one Democrats to nineteen Republicans). In state legislative contests, the pattern was similar: Democrats won control in two additional states for a total of twenty-five; Republicans retained control in eighteen states.[1]

Many factors have been cited to explain this unusual display of ticket-splitting: the "penance" vote whereby traditional Democrats, in casting what was perhaps their first ballot for a Republican presidential candidate, went out of their way to support all other Democrats on the ticket (indeed, John Connally's "Democrats for Nixon" pitch encouraged just this sort of ticket-splitting); President Nixon's decision not to campaign actively for other Republican candidates and the limited flow of campaign cash from national GOP coffers to Republican candidates; the unusually vigorous, and in most cases separate, campaigns conducted by most Democrats out of fear that they might be swept aside in the expected Nixon landslide; the tendency for congressional incumbents to be re-elected; the electorate's growing, perhaps instinctive, desire to restrain the exercise of presidential power by vesting control of the Congress in the opposition party; and, finally, the manner in which McGovern *himself* became the campaign's principal issue, making it easier for congressional and gubernatorial candidates to dissociate themselves from the controversial aspects of the presidential race, as well as easier for the voters to perceive a sharp distinction between the presidential contest and all others.

No doubt these factors, and many others unique to any given political contest, came together in varying combinations and permutations to shelter scores of seemingly vulnerable Democrats from the Nixon avalanche. Some, of course, weren't so fortunate: former Senator William B. Spong, Jr., of Virginia, for example, a clear favorite in September, probably would be back in Congress today if McGovern had not been the Democratic nominee.

It is not sufficient, however, to explain the Democratic Party's creditable performance below the presidential level simply on the basis of short-term factors unique to 1972. We must probe deeper for more basic trends, if they exist, by taking a more detailed look at how some Democrats, running in states or districts that seemingly should have been vulnerable in a Republican presidential landslide of the 1972 dimension, managed to defeat their GOP opponents—George McGovern's and Richard Nixon's campaigns and personalities notwithstanding.

From the early months of his presidential campaign in 1971, George McGovern built his candidacy around the notion of bringing government back to the people in an age of rising popular cynicism and alienation. One of the more monumental ironies of the Nixon-McGovern race, in a campaign filled with monumental ironies, was the public's judgment, as the survey data cited in Chapter 1 revealed, that Richard Nixon, not George McGovern, would make "the government pay more attention to the problems of the working man and his family" and that Richard Nixon, not George McGovern, would keep "the big interests from having too much influence over the government." [2] McGovern's poor showing helped produce the postelection belief among many persons that two key elements of his campaign—its emphasis on youth and its neopopulist appeal—were what the voters rejected. But an examination of congressional and gubernatorial races suggests that the very same appeals plainly helped to give many underdog Democrats their decisive edge in the voting booth.

First of all, the success of younger candidates in 1972 was striking. In fact, the Democrats retained their strong position in Congress because a number of younger candidates for the House and Senate defeated a number of older (in several cases ancient) Republicans. Of the six Senate seats that switched from Republican to Democratic control, all the Democrats were younger—in two cases more than twenty-five years younger —than their Republican opponents. The Democrats averaged 43.8 years of age compared to 58.7 years for the Republicans. The fourteen Democrats who won House seats previously held by Republicans—the critical factor in holding GOP gains in the House to twelve seats—averaged 40.8 years of age, to 45.4 years for the Republicans. In races where a Republican incumbent was running (as distinct from races where neither candidate was the incumbent), the age differential was even wider: 36.8 years for the Democratic challengers compared to 54.5 years for the Republican incumbents.[3]

The pattern of youthful success was not as clear in the gubernatorial races. Of the three governorships that Democrats captured from the Republicans, one Democrat was younger (Sherman W. Tribbit of Delaware), one was slightly older (Thomas P. Salmon, forty, of Vermont defeated Luther F. Hackett, thirty-nine), and one (Daniel Walker of Illinois) was the same age as his Republican opponent.[4]

Numerical age, of course, is no sure indication of a person's beliefs or political attitudes; ideological conservatism is hardly restricted to those of late middle age any more than practitioners of the New Politics are universally found to be under thirty. But it is significant that, in the races that were examined in more detail, the winning Democrats consciously stressed the attributes usually associated with youth—energy, enthusiasm, and sincerity, for example—and based their campaigns on the proposition that they would be more responsive, more active and more concerned than the Republican incumbents in representing their states and districts.

The trappings of the new populism were everywhere evident—two candidates criss-crossed their electoral constituencies (one a district, the other a whole state) on foot, for example—and all the winning Democrats placed considerable emphasis on projecting an image of sensitivity and responsiveness to individual needs in comparison to the Republican tendencies toward aloofness, ties to special interests of various sorts, and a general taking of one's constituents for granted.

Iowa: Nothing Helps a Fresh Face Like Good Organization

The Johnson landslide in 1964 helped elect five new Democratic congressmen from Iowa. One was John C. Culver, then thirty-two and recently resigned as Senator Edward Kennedy's legislative assistant, who defeated his Republican opponent by 8,100 votes (52 per cent). Realizing the immediate need to broaden his support before the 1966 congressional elections,

Culver sent his administrative assistant, Dick Clark, back to Iowa as full-time manager of his district office. Clark did his work well. Culver survived the Republican resurgence in 1966 (the other four Iowa freshmen were defeated) and decided to have Clark remain in Iowa on a full-time basis.

By 1970, Culver—with Clark's diligent assistance—had established his district as a safe Democratic seat, winning that year by 29,000 votes (60.5 per cent). By then, however, Clark had another assignment: to begin the preliminary organizational and political work that might culminate in a statewide race in 1972 against the incumbent Republican senator, Jack Miller. Clark, in turn, had plans of his own: to run for Culver's House seat if his boss decided to make the Senate race.

Clark traveled extensively in all sections of Iowa, assessing Culver's chances against Miller; he also set in motion, in collaboration with the state Democratic Party, an unprecedented canvass of Iowa homes, using a sophisticated voter-identification system whereby volunteers would telephone every home in a community, ask a series of questions to determine the political attitudes of the occupants, and decide whether or not they were potential Democratic—that is, Culver—supporters. This information was transferred to a computer for use in the 1972 campaign, in various ways, such as voter registration, sending computer letters, and compiling get-out-the-vote lists for Election Day. By all odds, it was the most professional organizational effort that Iowa Democrats had ever put together.[5]

As a consequence, it came as a surprise to observers when Culver decided not to oppose Miller after all and to run instead for re-election to the House. Some discouraging private polls, some personal reasons, and the apparent difficulty of raising money for a statewide campaign entered into Culver's decision that the risks in sacrificing his safe House seat for the chance of a Senate seat were too high, particularly in the questionable political conditions for Democrats generally in 1972.[6]

Clark, however, was in quite different circumstances: He

had already invested a considerable amount of energy and time in planning a campaign against Miller; he knew more than anyone else in Iowa about Miller and his vulnerabilities; he held no public office that would be lost by entering the race; and, when Culver backed out, none of the other possible Democratic candidates wanted the senatorial nomination. In these circumstances, Clark decided he had little to lose except some money and a half-year of his time. He accepted the challenge his boss turned down.

Once the choice for the Senate had been defined along lines favorable to Clark, the organization that had been built to help elect Culver was able to identify and turn out an extraordinary percentage of people just as ready to vote for Clark, as well as the rest of the state Democratic ticket.

Outside of the spadework he had personally done in behalf of Culver, Clark began the race with few obvious advantages and with manifold, seemingly insurmountable, problems. His name was practically unknown among Iowans, and he lacked the money to support a paid media campaign that could remedy the situation. His opponent was a well-known two-term senator, the ranking Republican on the Senate Agriculture Committee, who had carried every county in the state in 1966 and would not lack for campaign funds in 1972.

Clark decided to attack the recognition problem in a manner that leapfrogged the paid-media obstacle and simultaneously began to establish his down-to-earth populist credentials. He started walking from one end of the state to the other,. emulating the example of Democratic Senator Lawton Chiles of Florida in his winning 1970 campaign and the more recent effort of Wayne Owens, an equally unknown Democrat running for a House seat in Utah. In late June Clark set out on foot, walking from west to east, a trip that eventually took him into all sections of the state by early October. He logged 1,313 miles. In his frequent stops, he hammered away on a single theme: It's time the politicians got back to the people. The image of Clark hiking from town to town—an image that was increasingly transmitted by the local press and television along the way—dramatized this message with a directness and legitimacy that would have been difficult to duplicate with the most shrewdly designed paid-media campaign.

Once the general election campaign had started, Clark reinforced that image by pointing out specific incidents in Miller's Senate record that suggested favored treatment for a variety of special interests at the expense of the interests of the average Iowa voter. He criticized Miller's support for large agricultural corporations and food processors at the expense of the family farmer. He published complete lists of his own campaign contributions, repeatedly attacked Miller for refusing to reveal the sources of an estimated $200,000 in unreported contributions that were received before the campaign disclosure law became effective on April 7, and demanded that he explain an amendment he had offered to provide special tax treatment for a single insurance firm based in the Bahamas.

Miller refused to provide specific answers, and Clark simply repeated his charges and questions at every opportunity. When Miller sought to link Clark to the McGovern candidacy by implying that Clark was too liberal for Iowa, Clark responded that while he supported McGovern and intended to vote for him, the voters of Iowa had to decide who they wanted to represent them in the U.S. Senate. Miller's record of special interest legislation spoke directly to that choice; the McGovern presidential candidacy had nothing whatever to do with it, nor could the McGovern candidacy give substance to Miller's charge that Clark was excessively liberal. Clark limited his discussion of national issues to those that directly concerned Iowans, such as tax reform, the economy, and agriculture. McGovern came to Iowa on three occasions during the campaign; Clark appeared with him only once, at an evening rally at the Cow Barn in Des Moines.

Meanwhile, as Clark was keeping Miller on the defensive, thousands of volunteers were implementing the statewide Democratic voter identification program that Clark had started for Culver two years earlier. In the last three months of the campaign, 50,000 Democrats were registered, compared to 24,000 Republicans. Over the course of the voter-identification project, more than 60 per cent of the households in Iowa were called by telephone. In urban areas the Democrats recruited one volunteer door-knocker for every 100 households. By Election Day, a total of 350,000 likely Democratic households had been located; on Election Day, more than 2,000 of the state's 2,500 precincts had get-out-the-vote operations to make sure these Democratic voters went to the polls. Compared to the national voter turnout of 55 per cent, 68 per cent of registered Iowans voted. Most critical point of all: The Democratic strategists knew where their voters could be found and they got them to the voting booth—to the benefit of Clark and the state Democratic ticket generally.[7]

Miller simply failed to appreciate Clark's potential as a winner until it was too late. He spent much of his time in Washington and had little public visibility in Iowa until the closing weeks of the campaign. By then, he found himself solidly on the defensive, and his effort to portray his opponent as a McGovern radical never succeeded in impairing Clark's well-defined image as a politician who really cared about the people of Iowa.

On Election Day, it wasn't even close: Clark ran up a lead over Miller of 131,000 votes to win with 55 per cent. In the presidential balloting in Iowa, Nixon defeated McGovern by 210,000 votes—a 57.6 per cent victory.

COLORADO: RIPE FOR THE PICKING

Gordon Allott, sixty-two, conservative Republican from Colorado, was first elected to the U.S. Senate in 1954. It was a fairly narrow victory, but in 1960 and 1966 he won with increasing majorities.[8] It was assumed by everyone in Washington who thought about such things—including Allott—that he would be re-elected in 1972 without difficulty. He was, after all, one of the leading and most respected Republicans in the Senate. He was chairman of the Republican Policy Committee in the Senate, ranking minority member of the Committee on Interior and Insular Affairs, and a member of the Appropriations Committee. Any list of the half-dozen most important and influential Republicans in Congress would surely have included the name of Gordon Allott.

Floyd Haskell, fifty-six, a Colorado state legislator who switched from the Republican to the Democratic Party in 1970 in protest of President Nixon's invasion of Cambodia, knew something that Gordon Allott didn't. A private poll revealed that a lot of Colorado voters didn't fully understand how important Gordon Allott was in Washington; in fact, a lot of Colorado voters weren't sure who Gordon Allott was.

There is good reason for this: The size and composition of Colorado's electorate had changed considerably since Allott narrowly won his first Senate race eighteen years earlier. Allott, moreover, had never opened an office in the state. He spent most of his time in Washington, and had little interest in developing issues or legislation of particular interest to his changing Colorado constituency, preferring to deal with issues of national importance as one of President Nixon's most reliable spokesmen in the Senate. He was, in short, seriously out of touch with the Colorado electorate that would be voting in November 1972.

Given these conditions, a number of Democrats could have given Allott a close race in 1972, but most of the potential challengers assumed—along with Allott himself—that the senior U.S. senator from Colorado was unbeatable. Floyd Haskell thought otherwise and eventually won the party's nomination in a primary, even though the state Democratic convention had endorsed another Democrat. He then began implementing a simple, straightforward campaign strategy that was followed without deviation: Demonstrate an active and committed involvement with specific issues of immediate concern to Colorado voters—for example, land use planning, water diversion, taxes, preservation of Colorado beauty, the use of public funds for the Winter Olympics, the family farm—and in a manner that contrasted sharply with Allott's general aloofness and lack of concern.

A highly professional thirty-minute color documentary film —designed specifically to give voters a feel for Haskell as a man concerned principally with Colorado problems—was given heavy television exposure in all parts of the state. Radio commercials were used extensively: Forty-two different spots were produced, but, more significantly, thirty of them were targeted for use in specific locations, dealing with issues of special concern to the local area where they were aired. Haskell also planned each campaign day to ensure maximum possible exposure on local news programs, and his staff demonstrated considerable ingenuity in helping him carry out his plans. During a heavy snowstorm, for example, Haskell's aides took their boss on a round of the major Denver television stations in a four-wheel-drive Jeep to announce his filing of a law suit to force full disclosure of Allott's unreported campaign contributions. Since the stations' film crews had been immobilized by the blizzard, Haskell's announcement received an unusual amount of coverage—about ten minutes—on each station.

In the same way as Clark in Iowa, Haskell went to great lengths to portray his opponent principally as an advocate of special interests at the expense of the broader public interests of the citizens of Colorado. Allott's vote against the tax reform act of 1969, his refusal to disclose campaign contributions received prior to the effective date of the campaign disclosure law, his opposition to the eighteen-year-old vote, his ties to agribusiness, and his low ratings by environmental and conservation groups all received frequent attention from Haskell. He would conclude these specific attacks with a more general question: How has Allott's seniority in Congress or his position of influence with President Nixon helped the *people of Colorado?*

Allott, like his colleague Jack Miller, remained confident that things were well in hand until it was too late. Ten days before Election Day, Allott finally recognized the seriousness of Haskell's challenge, doubled the amount of paid commercials on television and radio, and arranged for a last-minute campaign stop by President Nixon. But a snowstorm forced the cancellation of Nixon's appearance, and Allott's television commercials came across as overly slick and distinctly out of character: Gordon Allott, the serious and reserved conservative, wearing a hard hat, or with a loosened necktie, or sitting on a lawn surrounded by young people. Toward the end of the campaign, Allott started talking about the "Mc-Govern-Haskell bunch" but Haskell either ignored the issue or simply remarked that McGovern wasn't running for the Senate from Colorado.

There was, however, a concerted effort among the Haskell staff to keep as much distance as possible between their Senate campaign and McGovern's presidential effort in Colorado. Haskell said he intended to vote for McGovern but did not agree with the South Dakotan on many of his more controversial positions. Despite the separate campaigns, Haskell did benefit from McGovern's well-organized get-out-the-vote operation on Election Day. (Unlike Clark in Iowa, Haskell did not attempt a major voter canvass or voter identification program). One campaign worker estimated that the McGovern forces brought to the polls voters who were against McGovern by a two-to-one margin but in favor of Haskell by the same ratio.

In many ways, Haskell conducted a far more traditional campaign in Colorado than Clark's in Iowa, and he was less consciously committed to developing an image as a fighting populist. It was not a campaign explicitly built around the theme of "returning government to the people." But there were important similarities: Haskell set out to convince the voters of Colorado that he differed from their influential Republican senator in being personally interested in their problems and the problems of the state. These concerns would receive his priority attention as a U.S. senator. Having determined early in the year that Allott was more vulnerable than anyone supposed, Haskell followed a strategy that exploited his opponent's major weaknesses—personal aloofness and ties to special interests—to the maximum degree possible. Allott, for his part, found it impossible to compensate for years of neglect of his Colorado constituency in the campaign's final days. He demonstrated once again the truth of the proposition that what wows political insiders in Washington, D.C., is likely to fall flat in Colorado Springs.

When the votes were counted, Haskell squeaked through to

a narrow victory, winning 49.4 per cent of the vote to Allott's 48.4 per cent, a plurality of 9,600 votes out of 905,000. Nixon rolled to a 267,000-vote lead over McGovern in Colorado— a whopping majority of 63 per cent.

GEORGIA: GO WHERE YOUR STRENGTH IS

In 1970, the Reverend Dr. Andrew Young, thirty-eight, former executive director of the Southern Christian Leadership Conference (SCLC) and one of Dr. Martin Luther King's most trusted associates, challenged the Republican incumbent, Fletcher Thompson, for the House seat from Georgia's 5th district, which encompassed most of Atlanta and its immediate suburbs. Young, a black, lost by 20,000 votes out of 137,000.

In 1972, Young ran again, this time against Rodney Cook, forty-eight—a Georgia state representative, former Atlanta alderman, and unsuccessful Atlanta mayoral candidate in 1969 —the Republican Party's nominee to succeed Thompson, who gave up his 5th district seat in what turned out to be an unsuccessful race for the U.S. Senate. Despite the obvious handicaps of a black former civil rights activist running for Congress in the year of the Nixon landslide from a Southern district where 62 per cent of the registered voters were white, Young won by 7,800 votes (again out of 137,000) and became the first black since 1871 to represent Georgia in the U.S. Congress.

The victory was a product of two major factors: political common sense and effective organization—avoiding issues that would either divide Young's potential supporters or arouse Young's likely opponents and focusing all organizational efforts in areas of greatest potential strength.[9] A private poll in August showed, for example, that Young was not looked upon with favor by white blue-collar workers or the middle-aged and older white groups, whereas among the young he did better against Cook.

The foundation for a winning campaign, however, had been laid in the previous two years through a series of reapportionment battles that eventually resulted in a congressional district slightly more favorable to Young and by Young's unceasing efforts after 1970 to broaden his appeal among both white and black voters. His position as chairman of the Atlanta Community Relations Commission provided an excellent base for these activities.

The first solid evidence of Young's increased political strength occurred in the primary contest to determine the Democratic nominee to oppose Cook in the general election. Young won convincingly with 60 per cent of the vote, defeating a young, moderate white member of the Atlanta Board of Aldermen and a vigorous, outspoken black alderman. Of particular interest was Young's improved performance over the 1970 primary: In 1972 he won 93 per cent of the black vote, compared to 76 per cent in 1970, and 32 per cent of the white vote, again an increase over 1970. The primary election also gave Young's campaign organization an opportunity to test the strategy that would be more fully implemented in the general election.

From the outset, the objective in the general election was clear: to secure the largest possible registration and turnout in the black community—38 per cent of the district's registered voters—and to hold Cook to no more than a three-to-one margin among the majority of white voters. But this, in turn, meant avoiding blatant and emotional appeals to blacks that would jeopardize the minimum 22-to-25 per cent of the white vote that Young needed to win. And it meant reaching the more moderate, middle-income elements of the white community without stimulating higher-than-normal voting participation among the generally hostile lower-income, blue-collar whites who might otherwise sit out the election.

Young's problem among black voters was complicated by the steady decrease in voter turnout among blacks that had taken place since a record-breaking 80 per cent voted in 1964 in the Johnson-Goldwater race. By 1970, in Young's first try for Congress, only 54.4 per cent of the registered blacks voted for congressman. A repetition of this performance in 1972, or a further decline, would put victory beyond reach.

Relying heavily upon neighborhood registration by volunteer deputy registrars, and persuading the Board of Elections to continue neighborhood registration when it was nearly ended well in advance of the deadline, the Young campaign added nearly 20,000 blacks in the 5th district. A lawsuit was filed to remove barriers to registration and voting in certain black precincts (such as having to cross an Interstate highway) that had resulted from the arbitrary drawing of precinct lines by the Board of Elections, with some black precincts split in half.

Just about every campaign tool that has ever been tried—door-to-door canvassing, phone banks, computer letters, sound trucks, neighborhood rallies, mobile bands on flatbed trucks, and spot commercials on black radio stations—were then used in black neighborhoods to stress the critical importance of getting to the polls on Election Day. In what turned out to be a critical service when a driving rain storm struck Atlanta on November 7, thirty-two transportation centers in the black neighborhoods helped bring Young's voters to the polls.

The increase in black participation was not spectacular—up a little more than two percentage points over 1970—but, for the first time in recent years, more blacks voted in the congressional race than voted for President, reversing the normal pattern of a 4-to-5 per cent dropoff between the two contests. The combination of these two factors brought victory within reach if Young could achieve the minimum of 25 per cent in the white community.

In planning their strategy for expanding Young's strength among white voters, his advisers decided to focus their campaign in selected white neighborhoods, such as Morningside, composed principally of younger, middle-to-upper-income white moderates, many originally from out of state, and to ignore the working-class neighborhoods in the southwest and southeast portions of the district. In other words, the realities of the Young campaign forced the Democratic candidate to rely heavily on what would normally be assumed to be a Republican-leaning constituency and generally to write off the traditional Democratic base of white lower-income workers.

In those white neighborhoods where it appeared sensible to campaign, volunteers began early in 1972 to call prospective voters by telephone and to identify Young supporters or potential supporters. This information eventually was used on Election Day in a low-key effort to encourage voting among whites known to favor Young's candidacy. Public endorsements from a number of respected white community leaders, such as former mayor Ivan Allen, Jr., made it more acceptable for other whites to acknowledge their backing of Young over Cook. A special computer letter for white voters under thirty was sent to every registered voter in this category. All of these activities were carried out with a minimum of fanfare and public exposure in order to limit the dangers of a backlash among those whites who, if aroused, would bitterly oppose the notion of a black congressman for Atlanta.

The effort to expand white support was complicated further by the appearance of a host of volatile issues that tended to divide the Atlanta community along racial lines, a split that could not be permitted to develop among Young's supporters. In the weeks immediately preceding the general election, everything seemed to go wrong—from a sudden flare-up in the protracted fifteen-year struggle to desegregate the Atlanta schools (including what was perceived to be court-ordered busing) and the fatal shooting of a white Internal Revenue Service supervisor by a black subordinate (Angela Davis promptly came to town) to labor disputes with racial overtones. Rodney Cook, generally viewed as a moderate on racial questions, could not let the busing controversy slip by, and it became one of his major campaign issues. He promised to fight for antibusing legislation in Congress, and his paid-media material included a photograph of Cook and Young with the caption: "What's the difference? . . . Plenty." Young responded by saying that he too opposed massive busing but that, if elected, he would not support federal antibusing legislation or a constitutional amendment to outlaw all busing under every circumstance.

Young's basic approach to these potentially explosive issues was to talk about subjects devoid of racial dimensions but of intense concern to the groups he needed for victory. Indeed, the most noteworthy aspect of Young's campaign was its dedicated, and successful, avoidance of issues that would generate uneasiness, if not overt hostility, in the white community. He could otherwise have lost much ground, for the August poll referred to earlier showed over one-third (39 per cent) of the voters in the 5th district agreeing with the statement: "I've heard that Andy Young has some radical positions"; 27 per cent disagreed, and 35 per cent had no opinion.

What, then, did Young talk about? In Morningside, one of Young's major sources of white support, he spoke out repeatedly against the construction of Interstate Highway 485, which would run right through the neighborhood. He appealed to conservationists by proposing the construction of a national park along the banks of the Chattahoochee River. In the small but influential Atlanta Jewish community, he stressed the plight of Soviet Jewry. Young talked about these issues with the quiet, sincere dedication that had served him so effectively during his years with SCLC and as chairman of the Atlanta Community Relations Commission. Without articulating this message explicitly, he projected an image of black-white cooperation on a broad range of concerns that touched the lives of 5th district voters. It was, in sum, an exercise in political common sense: to stake out relatively liberal positions on issues that would not split his potential supporters along racial lines and to avoid taking the initiative on those issues that would. And it worked.

It was, in many ways, a very traditional campaign. Young started early, worked hard, recruited volunteer help, registered voters, identified his potential voters, got his supporters to the polls on Election Day, and talked about issues that would attract, rather than scare away, the critical white votes that were needed for victory.

The original campaign strategy was achieved in all basic respects: In black precincts Young received 97.5 per cent of the vote, which had increased slightly over 1970; in white precincts he won 25.8 per cent of the vote, just over his projected minimum of 25 per cent; in racially heterogeneous precincts he received 64.2 per cent. Finally, Young outpolled McGovern in every precinct in the 5th district.[10]

UTAH: WE'LL DO IT OUR WAY, THANK YOU

Wayne Owens, thirty-five, worked for Edward Kennedy during the Senator's two years as the majority whip in the U.S. Senate. Following Kennedy's ouster from that post in 1970, Owens became administrative assistant to Senator Frank Moss of Utah and began thinking seriously of challenging Sherman Lloyd, fifty-eight, the incumbent Republican congressman from Utah's 2d district, which includes Salt Lake City and most of the state's western counties.

Lloyd, a moderately conservative Republican lawyer and former state legislator, had won his congressional seat easily in 1966 and was re-elected easily in 1968—both times winning 61 per cent of the vote. Expected again to win easily in 1970, Lloyd retained his seat but with a winning margin of only 52 per cent. Although he would still be the clear favorite in a race against a liberal ex-member of Ted Kennedy's staff, Lloyd's narrow margin in 1970 kept open the possibility of an upset. By the fall of 1971, Owens had decided to make the race; in February 1972 he resigned from Senator Moss's office to devote full time to his campaign.

Owens faced exactly the same two problems that initially confronted Dick Clark in Iowa: name recognition that bordered on zero (3 per cent in one early poll) and limited finances to support a media campaign that could remedy this weakness. Upon the urging of Senator Lawton Chiles, he settled on exactly the same solution: a two-month, 689-mile walk through his district. (Owens started walking on March 5, nearly three months before Clark set off across the highways of Iowa.)

But Owens's decision to walk the district was not reached without considerable discussion. Most of the party leaders in Salt Lake City opposed the idea if for no other reason than that Owens would spend seven weeks in the highly conservative southern portions of the district that contained a mere

8 per cent of the voting population—the hinterlands, to say the least. But Owens's immediate staff felt differently. They argued that, over time, word of his lonely trek through southern Utah would begin to filter north and make news; more important, he would be taking the essential first step in establishing an image of a young, active candidate concerned primarily with people and their problems. Owens started walking.

It was the first time that anybody running for Congress had bothered to visit many of the small towns in southwestern Utah. Preceded a day or two by a small advance team, Owens would arrive in a town, attend whatever small group events had been set up, and spend the rest of the day talking with citizens on the streets, in stores, and at lunch counters. As his staff had predicted, after several weeks of anonymous tramping by Owens, TV stations from the larger cities to the north began sending camera crews to cover the guy walking for Congress. The response of the voters was generally consistent: They disagreed with some of what Owens represented, particularly his opposition to the Vietnam War, but they recognized him as the first politician to come and listen to what they had to say. And this they liked.

In his talks, Owens concentrated on local issues, such as predator control, along with a general pitch on the inequities of the present tax system and the need for tax reform. But there was, in essence, one overriding issue in the Owens campaign from start to finish: How the government had lost communication with the people and how Owens would close this gap, at least for the people of Utah's 2d congressional district.

Following his nomination at the state Democratic convention in mid-June (he won 91 per cent of the delegate vote), Owens began a second walk, block by block, through populous Salt Lake County. Daily paid radio spots announced his presence in a given neighborhood and urged the residents to keep their eyes, and doors, open for "Wayne Owens, the walking congressional candidate." A team of volunteer walkers would work each neighborhood with Owens, fanning out on all sides, ringing door bells, handing out campaign literature, and telling residents that Owens would be on a certain street corner at a specific time if they wanted to meet him personally.

Again, the party leaders in Salt Lake City strongly advised Owens to spend more time in traditional campaign pursuits, such as making speeches before the major clubs and organizations. But Owens again rejected the advice and, with his volunteers, kept walking until they had covered all of Salt Lake County. A newspaper ad that appeared in that period summarized the Owens campaign: "Why am I walking for Congress? It's simply my way of applying for the job in person. . . . I have chosen to spend my campaign walking—listening to the people I will be representing."

Paid media ads—on television and in newspapers—kept to the same basic theme and projected visually the same image of Owens as a person concerned with people and their problems. In fact, most of the film footage used in Owens's commercials had been shot on the road during his initial walk through the southern reaches of the district. Only the most general statements about tax reform, education, employment, rising prices, and the environment appeared in the newspaper ads.

Owens generally kept away from the discussion of specific issues (after first being discouraged by the scant attention that detailed position papers attracted in the press and among most voters) and also refrained from personal criticism of his opponent, Sherman Lloyd. Almost totally ignored, Lloyd found few opportunities to counter Owens's growing momentum and the favorable exposure that Owens now received on a daily basis. Like Miller in Iowa, Allott in Colorado, and Cook in Atlanta, Lloyd attempted to link the candidacies of Owens and McGovern. Owens handled the issue somewhat differently from the other Democrats: He just ignored Lloyd and kept walking. There were seventeen joint appearances by the candidates, three on television, but they failed to shift the focus that Owens had established early in the campaign. A September newspaper poll showed that Owens was maintaining strong support among young voters without alienating blue-collar voters, a vital element in any Democratic victory in the 2d congressional district.

Although Owens and his volunteers walked in every neighborhood in Salt Lake County and in most of the smaller towns, they did not attempt to identify potential Owens supporters, as did Clark in Iowa and Young in selected Atlanta neighborhoods. Nor was there any get-out-the-vote effort on Election Day, keyed to specific homes. There was, however, extensive use of radio spots to boost voter registration, particularly among first-time voters. One spot simulated a news announcer on election night reporting that Owens had narrowly lost because too many young people had failed to register and vote. Owens's voice then cut in with the specifics on how young people could register in order to avoid such an outcome. On the final day of registration in Salt Lake County, 20,000 names were added to the lists, the largest number ever recorded on a single day. A similar saturation of Owens radio spots on Election Day urged people to vote.

Owens clearly touched a responsive chord among the voters of the 2d district, established a highly favorable image early in the campaign, and did nothing to cloud this image by venturing into the discussion of controversial issues. Lloyd, a rather cold and self-important Republican, simply was unable to cope with such a strategy, even in a fairly conservative state that gave Nixon a 68 per cent majority. When the votes were tabulated, Owens had won an impressive victory, 133,000 votes to 107,000 for Lloyd—a margin of 55–44 per cent.

VERMONT: KEEP IT SIMPLE AND STRAIGHTFORWARD

Tom Salmon, forty, initially a supporter of Senator Ed Muskie for the Democratic presidential nomination, ended up going to Miami Beach as one of Vermont's alternate delegates for McGovern, not what one would characterize as a power position in the national convention's pecking order. But for Salmon the big news at the convention wasn't McGovern's nomination; it was his own decision to return to Vermont and run for governor.

Having lost an earlier statewide race for attorney general, Salmon was one of about a half-dozen potential Democratic candidates for the governorship—all distinct underdogs to whomever the Republicans would nominate. An early poll to test their relative appeals showed Salmon trailing the eventual Republican candidate, Luther Hackett, by the rather decisive margin of 82–18 per cent. Not surprisingly, Salmon decided there were more profitable ways to spend his time than running for governor. He ended up as the last McGovern alternate to squeeze onto the Vermont delegation bound for Miami Beach.

The other Vermont Democrats who continued to eye the gubernatorial nomination were generating minimum interest and enthusiasm among even the hard core of the state's committed Democrats. Salmon, undaunted by the all-night sessions at Miami Beach and excited by what he perceived as the remarkable transformation of the Democratic Party, concluded that the political sidelines were no place for him. Even before leaving Miami Beach, he had changed his mind about running for governor. By the time of the Democratic primary in mid-September, the other possible Democratic candidate had dropped out and Salmon was on his way—right down to a resounding defeat, by every conceivable calculation.

The Republicans, however, were locked in a bitter struggle for the gubernatorial nomination, one that pitted the organization's choice, Luther Hackett, thirty-nine, the former majority leader in the Vermont house, against James Jeffords, the incumbent state attorney general (an office for which he had defeated Salmon decisively in the 1970 campaign). Vermont's popular two-term Republican governor, Deane C. Davis, personally endorsed Hackett as his chosen successor, and the Republican national committeeman from Vermont pitched in with a bitter personal attack against Jeffords. The state's well-oiled Republican machine was also used extensively to support Hackett's candidacy. In the end Hackett won, but at what turned out to be an excessively high price: Many moderate-to-liberal Republicans were outraged by the organization's treatment of Jeffords and ended up voting for

Salmon in the general election. Salmon suddenly found himself in the position of being able to conduct his campaign against the evils of Republican bossism and machine politics.

From mid-August to mid-September, while the Republicans were fighting it out and dominating the news media, Salmon traveled quietly around the state (not on foot), attending scores of local meetings, visiting with people, listening to their complaints—principally the rising property taxes and various threats to Vermont's environment—and establishing working ties with the more conservative elements of the state's Democratic Party. It was a time of listening to the voters and reminding them, on a person-to-person basis, that another candidate—Tom Salmon—would enter the field after the Republicans made their decision.

A poll taken after the September primary showed Salmon still far behind Hackett—67 to 33 per cent—and it was generally assumed that Hackett couldn't lose, especially in this strong Nixon year. In these circumstances, and with less than two months before Election Day, Salmon had no choice but to keep his campaign simple and direct, a campaign that everybody could understand the first time around.

Immediately after the primary, for example, while the Republicans were still rubbing their bruises, Salmon bought a series of paid television commercials that said, in essence: While the Republicans have been fighting for the nomination, I have been traveling the state listening to the people of Vermont. I don't think many Vermonters are satisfied with having to pay higher property taxes because real estate speculators and land developers have moved into our state. I'm for making them pay the higher taxes, not the people of Vermont. What does Luther Hackett propose? When Salmon suggested that no person pay more than 5 per cent of his or her disposable income on property taxes, he locked up this highly popular issue for the remainder of the campaign.

Hackett and the Republican national committeeman inadvertently gave Salmon his third major campaign theme: protecting Vermont's environment. Interrupting his postprimary vacation to address a meeting of mechanical engineers, Hackett. in response to a question from the audience, said he would support the repeal of Vermont's ban on nonreturnable containers, another way of saying he didn't mind if the Green Mountains were littered with soda and beer bottles. Salmon immediately announced his opposition to repeal, and Hackett was forced to admit his mistake and change his position. But the damage had been done. Vermont's environment was now an issue in the campaign.

The Republican national committeeman added to Hackett's problems by remarking in public: "Who are we saving the environment for, the porcupines?" Salmon promptly transformed that remark into the campaign's most dramatic illustration of how Hackett's election would directly jeopardize the preservation of the state's environment. He also assigned one full-time staff member to work with Vermont's many sporting and recreational clubs, stressing the importance of preserving open spaces and fighting land development projects by non-Vermonters.

Salmon offered no apologies about his support for McGovern, but his campaign was kept totally separate from the presidential effort. Although at one point the more radical McGovernites threatened to picket Salmon, a threat that was never carried out, he made his peace with most McGovern backers with the argument that McGovern was doomed in Vermont but that he himself still had a chance to win. The presence on the ballot of a radical left candidate, Bernard Sanders, permitted Salmon to assume the middle position on most issues and quieted the fears of the more conservative Democrats and moderate Republicans, whose support he needed. Salmon avoided national issues in favor of those local matters that clearly were having an impact on the voters: the way Hackett won the nomination, the issue of property taxes, the environment.

Hackett, for his part, grew increasingly arrogant and testy as Salmon's campaign began to catch fire. He diligently sought to link Salmon and McGovern and he emphasized his own ties with Nixon: "Nixon for America—Hackett for Vermont" appeared on television screens across the state. In the final weeks of the campaign, Salmon avoided all personal criticism of Hackett and Governor Deane C. Davis, even when Davis began attacking him personally.

By Election Day Salmon had managed to give the voters a

choice that few had believed possible less than two months
earlier: a vote for a young, attractive Democrat, the creature
of neither the left nor the right within the party, who had
staked out three highly effective issues, or a vote for a machine-
dominated, arrogant Republican, who seemed to believe that
the voters owed him the governor's chair.

Vermonters, like voters everywhere, didn't appreciate being
taken for granted by the Republican favorite. They elected
Salmon by the surprising margin of 105,000 votes to 82,000,
or 55–44 per cent, with 1 per cent for Bernard Sanders, the
radical leftist. In the presidential race, they stuck by Nixon,
who carried the state nearly two to one.

Lessons for 1974–76

It is admittedly a risky business to generalize from a limited
number of specific Democratic victories in congressional
and gubernatorial elections in 1972. There are always exceptions to which critics can point. Why, for example, did an
attractive young Texan, Barefoot Sanders, lose to incumbent
Senator John Tower, a Republican in considerable political
difficulties as 1972 began? Why did Senator Robert Griffin of
Michigan, an incumbent Republican who couldn't have
been in worse political shape in 1971, come through to a
relatively decisive victory over Democrat Frank Kelly, the
state attorney general? One reason, common to both races, is
the fact that Tower and Griffin, unlike Allott and Miller,
recognized their vulnerability and made efforts to repair the
damage well in advance of the campaign's final weeks. The
larger point is that every political contest contains its unique
dimensions that are quite distinct from all other contests in
a given election. Even a much larger sampling of 1972 races
would, in the end, fail to yield up anything approaching
absolute principles that could be applied generally by Democrats. But from the more modest perspective of searching for
insights and clues that might prove useful to the Democratic
Party as it approaches the elections in 1974 and seeks to re-
fashion a winning presidential coalition in 1976, what lessons,

if any, can be extracted from the five successful races of underdog Democrats?

The five races shared at least two common characteristics:
They began as probable, in several instances *almost guaranteed*, Republican victories, but each was lost to a Democrat;
four of the five Democrats were younger than their Republican
opponents (and Salmon of Vermont, although a year older
than his opponent, looked younger, acted younger, and was
generally thought to be younger). But the factor of numerical
age was far less important in these races than the vigorous
and imaginative campaigns waged by the Democratic candidates.

The campaigns themselves differed considerably in many
details. Each candidate reached a decision fairly early in the
race as to his own particular assets and his opponent's liabilities, developed a campaign strategy that played to these respective assets and liabilities, and adhered to this strategy with
minimum deviation until Election Day. In each case it was a
question of the Democrat's knowing what he wanted to accomplish in the campaign and succeeding.

This clarity and decisiveness contrast sharply with the
McGovern presidential campaign, in which general strategy
and lines of authority shifted constantly. The presidential
effort ended up being little more than a series of *ad hoc* im-
provisations from the successful campaign for the nomination—even though a preconvention strategy, by definition, is
almost certain to be insufficient to win a presidential majority
in the general election. As a consequence, the public's perception of McGovern as a man worthy of the trust and
responsibility of the Presidency became progressively more
negative as one campaign tactic after another was attempted,
evaluated, and abandoned before the public's eyes.

The five Democratic victors also spoke directly, and in
understandable and credible terms, to real needs of the
constituencies whose support they needed for victory. In this
regard, they shared McGovern's belief that a sizable portion
of the American electorate had become profoundly disen-
chanted with governmental structures at all levels—with their

seeming impersonality and unresponsiveness—and that the public would respond enthusiastically to a politician who demonstrated priority concern for individuals by listening to them, by taking their views seriously, and by giving direct attention to problems of immediate and personal concern. They steered clear of issues that seemingly contained the seeds of controversial social reform and that conjured up visions of radical change. They tapped the electorate's yearning for more responsive government without suffering the liabilities accumulated by McGovern in his presidential effort.

The five Democratic winners also had an extra something going for them. They were able to preserve the one ingredient essential to the execution of this highly personalized style of campaigning—personal trust. For some candidates the technique of walking across their state or district would have appeared artificial and unnatural—just as Gordon Allott came across as foolish wearing a hard hat or with a loosened necktie. But for Wayne Owens and Dick Clark the technique worked, primarily because it was, in fact, an opportunity for them to see their future constituents from ground level, so to speak, to learn directly about their problems and how as their elected representatives they could help. The legitimacy of the exercise went a long way toward establishing Owens and Clark as trustworthy people and created the necessary backdrop for the remainder of their campaigns.

Haskell, Salmon, and Young conducted campaigns that were less explicitly "populist" in tone but that focused, nevertheless, on highly visible issues of undoubted importance to large segments of the population in their states or districts—opposition to the Winter Olympics in Colorado, rising property taxes in Vermont, the construction of Interstate Highway 485 in Atlanta being explicit examples. Each gave priority to highly personalized campaigning, stressing direct contact with the voters where they lived, worked, shopped, and played instead of through organized rallies and set campaign speeches. Moreover, their campaign staffs had the ability to react quickly to events that would dramatize the candidate's concern for state and local problems. Salmon's people for example, learned of a proposal to begin strip mining in Orange County, Vermont, and within a day he had declared his total opposition to the plan. Hackett eventually took the same position, but he required three more days to do it.

All five candidates deliberately kept their campaigns simple, with a limited number of uncomplicated issues, an approach that produced two major benefits: The voters had little difficulty in figuring out what the candidates were saying, and the need for clarifications, retractions, and second thoughts was practically eliminated. The media usage of all five candidates reflected the same simplicity and directness.

Again, this approach contrasts sharply with the McGovern campaign. McGovern never succeeded in explaining his plan for providing every American with $1,000 in income supplements and eventually abandoned the proposal. His alternative defense budget, a worthwhile effort to illustrate a new concept in national security budgeting, unfortunately could not be explained simply and provided the Republicans with the kind of specifics that, taken out of context, were ripe for exploitation and misunderstanding.

Given the underdog position of all five Democrats at the start of their campaigns, each candidate exhibited a refreshing openmindedness about the voters to whom they could successfully appeal. Clark and Young went to considerable lengths to identify their potential supporters through telephone and door-to-door canvassing and then appealed directly to these voters for the balance of the campaign. Young found his election hopes resting, in part, on a socio-economic group traditionally assumed to be Republican. Owens spent eight weeks in the sparsely populated southern counties of the district that were filled with rock-ribbed conservatives. Salmon and Haskell made a special effort to appeal to moderate Republicans and independents.

In sum, none of the five candidates could assume that the traditional Democratic coalition of grade-school educated, blue-collar workers, union members, lower-income groups, minorities, intellectuals, and Catholics would be sufficient for them to win in their districts or states. And, interestingly enough, they did not limit themselves to traditional Democratic economic appeals or even to such highly popular issues as crime and drug abuse. The five candidates, all unapologetic Democrats, had no hesitation in designing their campaigns to appeal beyond the boundaries of what is conventionally thought to be the natural Democratic constituency. This necessarily meant adding to the basic bread-and-butter pitch certain appeals that were common to this wider cross-section of the electorate. The uniform success of such an effort in their five races suggests a proposition that will be examined in later chapters: As Franklin Roosevelt's New Deal coalition was held together primarily on grounds of economic self-interest, the development of noneconomic issues—including ways to make government more responsive and accountable to individual citizens—creates the potential today for Democrats to reach beyond the New Deal alignment to a broader constituency that cuts across traditional economic lines.

4

COALITION
AND IDEOLOGY:
LEGACY OF
PARADOX

R ichard Nixon won the Presidency in 1968 and 1972 even though his party was a distinct minority of the American electorate. It has been argued—most notably by Kevin Phillips and President Nixon himself—that these two presidential victories were the first signs of an "emerging Republican majority" or the "New American Majority," depending upon whose lexicon one selects.

Phillips argued that Nixon's only hope of victory in 1968 was to stitch together an electoral vote majority from the disgruntled and politically isolated. He urged that the GOP pay particular attention to groups such as the "sun-belt conservatives," the "backlash urban voters" and the "old South," the presumption being that once these voters abandoned their earlier Democratic and independent leanings in the presidential contest, they would move permanently into the Republican column in future nonpresidential elections. To date, no such thing has happened, and there are clear indications that it is not likely to happen in the foreseeable future.[1]

The euphoria of Phillips and Nixon arose in large part from the failure of the Democratic Party's 1972 presidential nominee to carry a majority of certain critical segments of the electorate on which the Democrats have counted since the days of Franklin Delano Roosevelt: the grade-school educated, blue-collar workers, Southerners, union members, and Catholics (see Table 7, below). But the Democratic Party's troubles in the presidential arena were presaged in 1968 when Hubert Humphrey—wounded by the third-party candidacy of George Wallace—dropped far below the levels achieved by Lyndon Johnson in his 1964 landslide and, more significantly, below John F. Kennedy's showing in his whisker-thin victory of 1960.

TABLE 7

PERCENTAGE PREFERRING DEMOCRATIC PRESIDENTIAL CANDIDATE

	1952	1956	1960	1964	1968	1972
Grade-school educated	52	50	55	66	52	49
Blue-collar workers	55	50	60	71	50	43
Those in households containing union member	61	57	65	73	56	46
Catholics	56	51	78	76	59	48
Southerners	51	49	51	52	31	34

If one is prepared to accept V. O. Key's proposition that "voters are not fools," then special attention should be given to his further admonition that "the popular majority does not hold together like a ball of sticky popcorn. Rather, no sooner has a popular majority been constructed than it begins to crumble." [2] Over the course of the 1960s, in other words, the political glue that held together this core of the Democratic Party's majority presidential coalition had been allowed to dry out. Even a full-fledged Democrat like Hubert Humphrey, openly appealing for their votes in 1968, could not rally sufficient numbers of the FDR coalition to win. George McGovern, often uncertain about both his party identification and his policy proposals, didn't stand a chance.

But these defections from the Democratic presidential column cannot hide an equally undisputed fact: The FDR coalition has not come apart at the seams. Not only have Democratic candidates done well in state races across the country, but a look at the population groups still supporting Democratic congressional candidates reveals impressive strength.

The best evidence of the demography of the reservoir of strength upon which the Democratic Party can draw in rebuilding a majority presidential coalition is found in a Gallup Poll of late September 1972. In this survey, registered voters were asked whether they would prefer to see a Democrat or a Republican win in their congressional district as well as their preference between McGovern and Nixon. On a nationwide basis, 50 per cent indicated a preference for a Democrat in Congress while only 32 per cent preferred McGovern over Nixon.

The results of this poll are summarized in Table 8 (below), which provides some very interesting information on (a) *Democratic voters* (those preferring a Democratic congressman); (b) *McGovern voters* (those preferring McGovern to Nixon); and (c) *defectors* (the proportion of Democratic voters deserting McGovern for Nixon).[3]

TABLE 8

	Democratic Voters [a] (per cent)	McGovern Voters [b] (per cent)	Defection Rate [c] (per cent)
Sex:			
Men	52	35	31
Women	49	29	40
Age:			
18–24	52	49	5
25–29	48	38	20
30–49	53	27	49
50 and over	48	30	37
Race:			
White	46	27	42
Nonwhite	89	74	18
Education:			
College	48	34	29
High school	49	28	42
Grade school	58	39	33
Region:			
East	54	40	26
Midwest	46	31	33
Deep South	52	24	53
Border	52	24	54
West	48	32	34

	Democratic Voters [a] (per cent)	McGovern Voters [b] (per cent)	Defection Rate [c] (per cent)
Household income:			
$15,000 and over	46	27	40
$10,00–$14,999	52	30	42
$7,000–$9,999	48	26	47
$5,000–$6,999	49	36	26
$3,000–$4,999	54	37	31
Under $3,000	59	43	27
Occupation of head of household:			
Professional/business	47	28	39
White collar	44	30	33
Skilled worker	52	25	51
Unskilled worker	61	39	37
Farmer	42	19	54
Non–labor force [d]	48	36	24
Religion:[e]			
Protestant	42	25	41
Catholic	61	39	36
Locality Size:			
1,000,000 and over	62	44	28
500,000–999,999	49	32	36
50,000–499,999	55	35	36
2,500–49,999	43	27	37
Under 2,500	41	22	47
Union affiliation:			
Union household	65	40	38
Nonunion household	46	29	36

[a] Percentage preferring a Democrat to win the local congressional election over a Republican or other party candidate.

[b] Percentage preferring McGovern over Nixon in standard Gallup "trial heat."

[c] The difference between "Democratic voters" and "McGovern voters" as a percentage of "Democratic voters."

[d] Mostly retired persons.

[e] Too few cases of Jews for statistically meaningful percentages.

This table suggests a couple of important things. First, it is evident that significant percentages of traditionally Democratic segments of the electorate still indicated a preference for a Democratic congressman from their district, even though they were less than enthusiastic about McGovern. Second, it points up those areas of greatest defection from the Democratic fold and illustrates that the highest rate of defection came in the border states and Deep South (54 and 53 per cent) closely followed by the rates of farmers, skilled workers, the middle-aged (49 per cent) and upper and middle-upper income groups (40 and 47 per cent). Only among Democratic young people (18–24 years) did the defection rate fall below 10 per cent.

Although one cannot help but be impressed with the breadth of Democratic defections from the McGovern candidacy, the lesson to bear in mind is that defections in one or two presidential elections do not necessarily mean permanent desertions. As illustrated by Table 9 (below), Democratic Party identification has remained relatively stable over the years. The McGovern candidacy did account for an increase in independent leanings and a drop in Democratic loyalties prior to the 1972 election, but the balance promptly shifted back to a more normal pattern in January 1973. As President Nixon's troubles with the economy and Watergate multiplied, the GOP lost strength and, once again, the independents principally gained.

TABLE 9

PARTY IDENTIFICATION [4]

| | (percentages of samples) | | |
	Democrat	Republican	Independent
1939	42	38	20
1945	44	36	20
1950	45	33	22
1953	44	37	19
1960	47	30	23
1965	49	25	26
1970	45	29	26
1972 (October)	38	30	32
1973 (January)	42	27	31
1973 (September)	43	24	33

The most noticeable shift over the long term has been from Republican to independent—a shift of 11 percentage points in the course of three decades, 1939–73. This does not necessarily mean that Republican losses were direct gains for independents, but as Table 10 shows it does illustrate the general trend away from the Republican Party.

TABLE 10

	1939 (per cent)	1973 (per cent)	Shift
Democrat	42	42	—
Republican	38	27	— 11 pct. pts.
Independent	20	31	+ 11 pct. pts.

These gross figures mask important shifts, such as the loss of many Democratic loyalists in the South. As of 1973, however, these voters had not moved to the Republican column —only to independent status. In no region of the country was there a significant gain for the GOP. (See Table 11.) Another noteworthy shift has been the desertion since 1939 of a sizable number of business and professional people from the Republican Party. (See Table 12.) This was the constituency that, for example, played a significant role in Andrew Young's victory in Georgia's 5th congressional district, as discussed in Chapter 3. In 1939, nearly half (46 per cent) of this group looked upon themselves as Republicans; thirty years later, the figure had dropped to less than a third (32 per cent).

TABLE 11

REGIONAL SHIFTS FROM 1939 TO 1973 (PERCENTAGE POINTS) [5]

	Democrat	Republican	Independent
East	+ 8	— 15	+ 7
Midwest	— 2	— 11	+ 13
South	— 23	+ 2	+ 21
West	+ 1	— 7	+ 6

TABLE 12

OCCUPATIONAL SHIFTS FROM 1939 TO 1973 (PERCENTAGE POINTS) [6]

	Democrat	Republican	Independent
Professional & business	+ 3	— 14	+ 11
White collar	— 7	— 4	+ 11
Manual worker	...	— 14	+ 14
Farmer	— 8	— 6	+ 14

These data, taken together, reveal the nature of the Democratic problem, as well as hold out hope that the problem is not beyond solution: Although the Democratic Party has suffered serious defections among critically important population groups in the contest for the Presidency, the party's base among the voters remains strong at the state and congressional level. Moreover, while the party's traditional base among the grade-school educated, union members, blue-collar workers, Catholics, and Southerners—the guts of the New Deal coalition—has eroded in the last two presidential elections, other evidence indicates new inroads by the Democrats among better-educated, upper-income voters. These shifts are part of the continuing process of voter realignment that takes place in every election, as millions of individuals decide how their interests and concerns can be advanced most effectively in the voting booth. But the conventional wisdom that the *party* has suffered a critical net loss of support among the electorate is simply incorrect.

On the other hand, the longer-term trend away from both major parties to independent status should eliminate any premature complacency for the Democrats, not to mention the GOP. As the five cases in Chapter 3 illustrated, however, these independents are quite receptive to Democratic appeals that emphasize a candidate's competence and his responsiveness to constituent interests. It is also true that independents—a firm majority of whom usually vote Republican and consider themselves "conservatives"—are generally receptive to economic appeals that stress the needs of the average citizen as opposed to the interests of "big business"—the kind of message that Democrats should be better able than Republicans to deliver.

Voters make judgments about candidates and their programs that, in combination with more stable factors like party identification, are ultimately expressed in the ballot box. A party seriously concerned about winning elections—and, more significantly, about governing *after* the election—thus has to have some clear notions of what the public considers to be sensible and effective ways of running the country.

To be more specific: The voters' negative judgment of the competence and executive personality of the Democratic candidate in 1972, discussed in Chapter 1, to a lesser degree accounted for a portion of Hubert Humphrey's troubles in 1968. Mixed in with these concerns, however, are indications that certain of the governmental strategies on which the Democrats have relied since the days of Franklin Roosevelt have lost much of their potency on Election Day. For Democrats in the mid–1970s, this would seem to call for a re-examination of the assumptions that have guided their actions on the national level for two generations and a reshaping of the appeals that Democrats bring to the voters at election time.

Gary Hart, Senator McGovern's youthful campaign director, spoke to the ideological difficulties encountered in the 1972 campaign in his book:

> The traditional sources of invigorating, inspiring, and creative ideas were dissipated. The best thinkers of the 1930s, 40s, and 50s and even the 1960s were not producing. Whether this resulted from age, depression, frustration at the nation's ponderous rate of progress, or lassitude, the results were crystal clear: by 1972, American liberalism was near bankruptcy.[7]

Well, perhaps, although it all depends on what you mean by "liberalism"—a problem we shall examine briefly in the next pages. The more immediate fact is that "liberals"—however defined—today occupy the smallest portion of the American electorate: In a recent Gallup Poll, for example, slightly more than one-fifth (23 per cent) of the people considered themselves "liberal," 41 per cent "conservative," and 31 per cent "middle-of-the-road." [8] The trend since 1970, however, has been toward a small growth of the liberal and conservative ends of the ideological spectrum at the expense of the middle, especially for the Democrats (see Table 13). In this period the percentage increase of Democratic conservatives (6 per cent) has been twice as large as the increase of liberals (3 per cent). It seems fair to say that liberalism reflects the attitudes of less than one-third of the Democratic constituency and cannot, by itself, provide the ideological base for building a national majority coalition. But neither can the Democrats afford to lose those voters who consider themselves liberals. This is the core of the Democratic Party's ideological dilemma.

TABLE 13

	Conservative	Middle-of-the-road	Liberal	Don't Know
		(percentages)		
January 1973:				
NATIONAL AVERAGE	41	31	23	5
Democrats	36	30	29	5
Independents	38	34	25	3
Republicans	53	30	13	4
October 1970:				
NATIONAL AVERAGE	40	35	20	5
Democrats	30	38	26	4
Independents	34	38	24	4
Republicans	57	30	10	3

Walter Dean Burnham, in a memorandum to his MIT colleagues written prior to the 1972 elections, argued that the basis for what he calls "interest-group liberalism"—a reliance on federal activism to sustain the political loyalties of various economic and social groups—has disappeared, and with it the ideology that has guided Democratic thought and action since the New Deal.[9] He wrote that "the United States is passing through one of the deepest transitional crises in its history," and that "the crisis has increasingly assumed the form of a crisis of political legitimacy." The four underlying factors that brought about this crisis he identified as:

- Economic pressures arising from the dual problem of inflation in the midst of stagnation, coupled with the long-term deterioration of the international competitive position of the American economy
- Profound changes in the American class structure that arise when persons are separated into the technologically competent, the technologically obsolescent, and the technologically superfluous, and when these divisions are

superimposed on the more traditional patterns of industrial stratification
- Massive changes in where people live: the technologically
superfluous, for example, being herded into the central
cities, and the technologically obsolescent and technologically competent heading to the suburbs, coupled
with a continuing shift of population to the West and
the newly industrialized South
- Major cultural ruptures between generations, occupa-
tions, and education-income levels

Taken together, these changes, in Burnham's view, have
undermined the basis of the old New Deal alignment and contributed to the bankruptcy of the interest-group liberalism
that represented the New Deal's ideological thrust. The attack
on the FDR ideology has come from two directions: those
who seek a moral regeneration of the political process and,
curiously enough, a major expansion of domestic activities
along Great Society lines (the New Politics) and those who
resist what they regard as excessive federal help to the poor in
order to stem runaway taxation and inflation (the "New
American Majority").

From Burnham's perspective, "a popular settling of ac-
counts with interest-group liberalism is still going on; it is
still the unfinished business." And because so many of the
visible and articulate spokesmen of interest-group liberalism
have been identified as comprising the political establishment
of the last two generations, Nixon, the presidential incumbent, could picture himself as the champion of the antiestab-
lishment forces. To quote Burnham again:

> . . . we see the extraordinary spectacle of an incumbent running for
> re-election and being re-elected in a time of vast, pervasive dis-
> content; an incumbent running as a kind of underdog against an
> "establishment" that he somehow—despite his incumbency—is able
> to identify with his opponent.

Despite McGovern's failure at the polls and his identification with the forces of the New Politics, Burnham's analysis

suggests that, to the extent the Democratic Party simply attempts to regroup its forces around traditional concepts of interest-group liberalism, it is bound to fall short of being an effective political force. In his words, "one very important truth of American politics is that activist liberalism repeatedly crashes against the outer limits of what the system can provide without fundamentally changing liberalism's character or beneficiaries, and so regularly comes to grief."

But a question arises: If the basis for the old New Deal alignment has been undermined by the social changes cited, why do Democrats continue to win at the congressional and state levels? It could, of course, be a matter of time lag: As Phillips and Nixon argue, it takes a few elections for the shifts at the presidential level to filter down to congressional and state races. But it could also be that congressional and state Democrats have been more skillful in adjusting their political beliefs and actions to social change, better able to retain the loyalties of "casual Democrats" who deserted McGovern in droves, better able to recruit the support of persons not normally thought to be Democrats, and better able to duck the divisive national issues that dogged the political footsteps of Humphrey and McGovern.

The Democrats are unlikely to remain satisfied with a long-term lease on Capitol Hill if they keep receiving no-vacancy notices at the White House. Yet the transformation of a congressional majority into a presidential victory can be difficult, especially if familiar ideological guideposts can no longer be relied upon as clues to political success. Clearly, the FDR ideology is in trouble—under the gun from both left and right, as seen in public opinion polls and in the ideological struggle within the Democratic Party between the defenders of the New Deal and the advocates of the New Politics. Neither view within the party offers much hope of addressing national problems in a way that can build a presidential majority capable of effective political leadership. Nor does either view face up to the harsh realities that arise in *governing* the nation today—not only from the perspective of Congress but also from the Oval Office in the White House.

As the Nixon Presidency struggles to survive the seemingly
endless disclosures of official deception and wrongdoing, Democrats still face the difficult job of defining a new governing
strategy to guide their actions in what is likely to be a
chaotic future for everyone. This requires, in turn, a political
ideology that reflects the values and beliefs of the American
people and that is faithful to the party's traditional concern
for social justice and human rights.

The definition of that ideology is neither an easy nor a
self-evident undertaking. But the process must begin with a
fresh look at three fundamental problems that are, or should
be, at the core of contemporary American political discussion
—the level of federal activism, the nature of the federal system, and the problem of racial justice. It must also take into
account two issues of intense political impact—what we shall
call the economic issue and the social issue. How can Democrats deal effectively, both politically and governmentally, with
these matters? Is a workable ideology for Democrats possible
to achieve?

THE IDEOLOGICAL-OPERATIONAL SPLIT

It was in 1964 that Lloyd A. Free and Hadley Cantril first
highlighted public ambivalence about the role of the federal
government in solving the nation's domestic problems. In a
survey just prior to the 1964 election, they presented a national cross-section of the public with two batteries of questions. One battery consisted of a series of propositions couched
in essentially ideological terms: "The federal government is
interfering too much in state and local matters"; "the government has gone too far in regulating business and interfering
with the free enterprise system"; "generally speaking, any able-
bodied person who really wants to work in this country can
find a job and earn a living"; and the like.[10] The second battery of questions dealt with public attitudes toward specific
federal programs: aid to education, medicare, low-rent public
housing, urban renewal, and so on.[11]

At the level of ideology, Free and Cantril found the public

was generally opposed to an extensive, activist role for the federal government. But when it came to specific governmental programs—the operational dimension—the public was overwhelmingly in support of a strong federal role. The researchers constructed two indices, each summarizing the patterns of each respondent's answers—one index for the ideological battery of questions, one for the level of programmatic or operational support. Respondents were then classified along a continuum from "liberal" to "conservative." Table 14 shows the results. Half of the public fell toward the conservative side on the ideological battery of questions while two-thirds came out on the liberal side in the operational, or programmatic, battery of questions.[12]

TABLE 14

	Ideological Level		Operational Level	
	(percentages)			
Completely liberal	4	} 16	44	} 65
Predominantly liberal	12		21	
Middle-of-the-road	34		21	
Predominantly conservative	20	} 50	7	} 14
Completely conservative	30		7	
	100		100	

Highlighting this ambivalence even further was the finding that nearly half (46 per cent) of those who qualified as "conservatives" ideologically *also* qualified as "liberals" at the level of operational support for specific governmental programs.[13] Free and Cantril thus concluded: "While the old argument about the 'welfare state' has long since been resolved at the operational level of government programs, it most definitely has not been resolved at the ideological level."[14]

To explore this political schizophrenia further, a special survey was commissioned for this book through the Gallup Organization. Interviews were conducted with a national cross-section over the weekend of January 26–28, 1973.[15] First, the survey checked the extent to which the ideological-operational ambivalence found in 1964 was still part of the American political psyche by repeating two of the same questions (see

Table 15). The public's view, it can be reported, is as inconsistent as ever.

TABLE 15

Statement: "Generally speaking, any able-bodied person who really wants to work in this country can find a job and earn a living." Percentage answering:

	1964	1973
Agree	76	79
Disagree	21	20
No opinion	3	1

Statement: "The federal government has a responsibility to try to do away with poverty in this country." Percentage answering:

	1964	1973
Agree	72	74
Disagree	20	21
No opinion	8	5

In political terms, the argument is joined on the question of government spending. Never one to shy away from exploiting to the fullest the public's inherent ideological conservatism, President Nixon, emboldened by his perceived mandate on Election Day, 1972, issued a seemingly nonstop stream of White House pronouncements in early 1973 that the American people were fed up with "paternalism" and subscribed enthusiastically to the "work ethic," not the "welfare ethic." "Ask not what government can do for you," he proclaimed in his second Inaugural Address, "ask what you can do for yourself."

Not surprisingly, when the issue is cast in general ideological terms, there *is* significant public support for the contention that there is too much government spending. In the special January survey, 66 per cent of the public agreed that "we should hold the line on federal spending by cutting back on certain government programs—even those that many people think are important."

But when the issue is presented in terms of specific social programs, the same high level of public support for government spending that existed in 1964 is again expressed—Nixonian rhetoric notwithstanding. In June 1972, in their study for Potomac Associates, Lloyd Free and William Watts asked respondents their opinions in nine areas of social spending. Among other questions, respondents were asked in relation to each area "whether you feel the amount of tax money now being spent should be increased, kept at the present level, reduced, or ended altogether." In only one instance—welfare programs to help low-income families—was the proportion favoring reduction or termination of a specific program more than *one-fifth* of the public (see Table 16). The vast majority favored spending at the present level if not actually increased spending.[16]

TABLE 16

	In-creased	Present Level	Re-duced	Ended Alto-gether	No Opin-ion
			(percentages)		
Federal programs to help elderly people, for example, by increasing the social security payments they receive	74	21	2	—	3
Federal programs to improve the education of children from low-income families	62	28	3	2	5
Federal programs to make a college education possible for young people who could not otherwise afford it	54	32	7	4	3
The medicaid program to help low-income families pay their medical bills	52	35	6	2	5
Programs to rebuild run-down sections of our cities	52	29	11	5	3
Programs to provide government-paid jobs for the unemployed	48	31	10	5	6
Federal programs to help build low-rent public housing	40	40	12	4	4
Programs to help improve the situation of black Americans	33	43	11	7	6

TABLE 16 *(continued)*

	In-creased	Present Level	Re-duced	Ended Alto-gether	No Opin-ion
			(percentages)		
Welfare programs to help low-income families	30	41	18	6	5
Average for the nine problem areas	49	33	9	4	5

Even in relation to the two problems at the bottom of the list—programs to help black Americans and welfare—about three-fourths of the public approve at least the present level of federal spending. In summary terms—that is, averaging the responses for the nine program areas—82 per cent of the public favors federal spending at the present level or better. Nearly half on the average support *increased* spending.

This point will be developed more fully in the next chapter, but it is clear that the Democratic Party is less vulnerable on the government spending issue than many persons thought, as long as the debate is not waged in the language of ideological conservatism.

Prior to the furor over Watergate, President Nixon had gone a considerable distance toward his goal of establishing in the electorate's mind the bald choice between accepting the spending limits he proposed to Congress or the inevitability of higher federal taxes, more inflation, or both. He had carefully sidestepped any serious discussion of alternative ways to acquire money for government purposes: tax reform or re-ordering national priorities. Both continue to merit attention as Democratic responses to the antispending ideological offensive.

As reported in Chapter 1, in mid-October 1972, despite Senator McGovern's poor showing in the polls, the balance of opinion sided with his position that the way to hold down taxes was not to cut back on federal spending but to close tax loopholes. In the special Gallup survey of January 1973, 77 per cent of the public agreed with the statement that "the large corporations and wealthy people should be made to pay a greater share of the tax burden." In fact, 78 per cent of those who favored holding the line on spending by cutting back on federal programs also felt that the corporations and rich are getting an unfair tax break. Tax reform apparently remains an issue with long-term political appeal.

The public is probably more than a little bored with the annual ritual of congressional Democrats repeating their rote demands for a reordering of national priorities, at least in the terms in which the debate has been cast for the last decade. Nonetheless, the January 1973 survey disclosed that 61 per cent agreed that "we are spending more money than necessary for our military defenses that should be spent for things like improving education, fighting crime, and eliminating pollution."

This kind of direct trade-off between the level of defense spending and money for various domestic programs must be handled gingerly, however. In *State of the Nation,* Watts and Free found that 49 per cent of the public called for the same amount of defense spending as at present, or more, while 42 per cent wanted defense spending reduced or ended altogether. Moreover, 78 per cent believed either that the national defense is not strong enough (27 per cent) or is about right (51 per cent).[17] These results help explain John Connally's success, and the success of the "Democrats for *Nixon*" spot commercials, in demolishing McGovern's personal credibility on the defense issue through vivid, if misleading, dramatizations of the military impact of his alternative defense budget. The 1972 campaign should remind Democrats of the extreme sensitivity of the national-priorities issue if it appears to involve an unacceptable weakening of our defense capability.

But if the issue of reordering national priorities is redefined, at least partially, to mean changes in the way government goes about its business—who benefits and who sacrifices at a given level of government activity—the potential for public support improves, the pitfalls of the defense issue are avoided. and the issue is recast in terms more likely to attract and hold the public's attention. We have already seen how the voters in five races responded positively to appeals that stressed greater personal concern by elected officials for individual problems and needs. In the *State of the Nation* study, respondents were asked to rate "government in general" in a number of respects. The sizable negative ratings are significant: 65 per cent give an unfavorable rating to government when it comes to "responsiveness to the needs of the people"; 61 per cent rate the government as inefficient; and 57 per cent give a low rating on "honesty and fairness." In fact, Watts and Free found a majority (54 per cent) feeling that "basic changes will be needed in the way government is set up"; 36 per cent disagreed, with 10 per cent having no opinion.[18]

To sum up: (1) The Democratic Party need not shy away from the advocacy of specific federal programs just because of Republican sallies that the average taxpayer will be the loser, particularly if such tax reform as the closing of loopholes is advanced as one solution to the revenue problem. (2) But Democrats must be careful to keep their advocacy of social programming to the level of specific problem areas and related to specific needs that people can understand, remembering that the more personalized the appeal, the better will it be received. (3) Broad philosophical propositions about the importance of federal activism should be avoided since they are likely to clash head-on with the public's entrenched ideological conservatism.

When George McGovern forgot this lesson in 1972, it was a curious reversal of Barry Goldwater's failure in 1964 to appreciate the disasters that awaited any candidate who proposed the destruction or modification of specific federal programs like TVA and social security—a posture that ignored the public's equally firm commitment to operational liberalism.

THE ISSUE OF DECENTRALIZATION

An integral element of the New Deal ideology has been the primacy of the federal government in dealing with the nation's most important domestic problems. This tenet was directly challenged by President Nixon early in his second term. He set the tone in his Inaugural Address: "We have lived too long with the consequences of attempting to gather all power and responsibility to Washington. Abroad and at home, the time has come to turn away from the condescending policies of paternalism—of 'Washington knows best.' "

Instead of federal programs that establish guidelines and standards for state and local governments as the price for federal money, Nixon proposed a combination of general and special revenue sharing that vested more operational responsibility with state and local authorities, along with far greater operational flexibility. Congressional Democrats and others have raised certain questions about the competence and commitment of state and local authorities to assume this burden. Can they stand firm against the predictable local pressures to forget about the more urgent and difficult domestic problems—educational inequality, housing deficiencies, poverty, welfare reform, and the like? Do state and local governments have the competence and integrity to deliver more adequately across the board than the federal government? Is not decentralization of the problem-solving effort merely a way to wash the federal government's hands of a number of long-term, seemingly intractable issues?

These are serious questions. They reflect not only the concern that many of the party's major domestic commitments of the past generation will be jeopardized, but the predictable Democratic reaction to a Republican strategy that runs directly counter to the Democratic Party's controlling ideology since the days of the New Deal. Yet the Democratic Party must avoid being placed on the defensive, locking itself into an unthinking opposition to the retooling of governmental institutions through the decentralization of functions. As David Broder wrote in the *Washington Post* in January 1973:

> Instead of the Republicans playing their traditional part as defenders of the status quo, they have seized—through Mr. Nixon—the banner of change. And instead of the Democrats talking innovation and progress, as they have usually done, they are . . . vowing to defend what they have created in the past 40 years. Given the state of public opinion concerning Washington and its

works, it takes no genius to figure out which party is going to come up on top in that fight. Resistance to change is the sure ticket for political oblivion.

Looking somewhat more precisely at the "state of public opinion concerning Washington and its works," various data suggest a continuing and curious ambivalence among the electorate about the proper role of the federal goverment in dealing with current problems. On the one hand, as reported by the Harris Survey released May 28, 1973 (see Table 17), there has been a marked decline in the public's confidence in all branches of the federal government since the mid-1960s.

TABLE 17

Percentage expressing "great deal of confidence" in:	1973	1966	Decline
U.S. Supreme Court	28	51	—23
Executive branch	27	41	—14
Congress	21	42	—21

But the public also believes that decisions made at the federal level are more likely to affect them personally in "very important" ways than decisions made at the state and local level, as Table 18 shows.

TABLE 18
IMPORTANCE OF GOVERNMENTAL DECISIONS PERSONALLY

Percentage answering:	Federal	State	Local
Very important	64	47	47
Somewhat important	21	35	26
Slightly important	7	10	17
Not important at all	2	2	5
Not sure	6	6	5

Does this mean that the public supports a massive transferal of governmental responsibility from the federal to the state and local level?

To get at the answer to this question, the January 1973 survey conducted for this book by the Gallup Organization asked: "On this card are listed a number of problems some people would like to see handled primarily by the federal government in Washington and other people would like to see handled primarily by state and local government. Which ones do you, yourself, feel should be handled by state and local government? Name as many or as few as you wish." [19]

Table 19, below, shows that the federal government remains an important source of decision and action in a number of problem areas, including poverty, health care, race relations, consumer affairs, pollution, and housing. Problems better handled by state and local authorities include crime and lawlessness, the quality of education, unemployment, and drugs and drug addiction.

TABLE 19

PROBLEMS BETTER HANDLED BY STATE AND LOCAL GOVERNMENT

	Per cent
Crime and lawlessness	62
Improving the quality of education	53
Unemployment and lack of job opportunities	49
Drugs and drug addiction	44
Providing better housing	39
Problems facing the elderly	39
Water and air pollution	38
Protecting the buying public from being cheated	36
Racial tensions	35
Providing more adequate health care and medical services	34
The problem of poverty	29
None of these	2
No opinion	3

The public's loss of confidence in the federal government and its recognition of the importance of federal decisions apparently have not caused a corresponding movement to shift the burden of government activity to the state and local level. In his May 28, 1973, survey, quoted above, Harris asked a similar question and found that in eight out of the eleven policy areas asked about, the public "tends to see the federal responsibility as the primary one." [20] This suggests that Democrats can look to the public for at least qualified support in

opposing any *across-the-board* decentralization of governmental functions: Sizable portions of the electorate still look
to Washington in such important areas as poverty, health
care, consumerism, housing, and the like.

To obtain a general and admittedly rough sense of those
population groups most likely to favor decentralization of
federal activities, respondents in the January 1973 survey were
scored as to how many items on the card—that is, governmental activities—they selected as being better handled by
state and local governments. For analytical purposes, persons who selected four or more items on the card were classified as favoring decentralization, and persons who selected
fewer than four were grouped together as "anti-decentraliza-
tion." A total of 44 per cent of the sample selected more than
four items.

A number of surprises were forthcoming from this analysis,
among them: (1) There is little difference among Democrats,
Republicans, and independents in the desire to see federal
activities decentralized. (2) There is little difference between
those who approve of the job Nixon is doing as President and
those who disapprove. (See Table 20.)

Regional differences also appear: Those in the South are
most favorable to decentralization, those in the East least
favorable. The significant differences by educational level, with
the least-educated most opposed to decentralization, perhaps
can be explained, at least in part, by the reticence of the less-
educated, who selected a few token items from the card but
did not discriminate as completely as the better-educated
among the items listed—but may also reflect the greater reliance that the less-educated place on the federal government
in their hopes for a better life.

The most important finding is that there were *no* significant
differences along the lines of party preference or attitude
toward Richard Nixon as President when it came to the matter of decentralizing government functions. This general attitude supports the notion that Democrats should avoid a posture of total opposition to the Nixon reorganization proposals.
However, the public clearly appreciates the vital role that the

federal government must continue to play in many problem areas, and its attitude on this matter is not unlike what prevails on the question of federal spending. That is, at the ideological level the public can appear quite conservative, with "big government," Washington bureaucrats, and red tape inevitably generating high levels of public indignation, but for dealing with real problems—building houses or fighting pollution, for example—the average citizen appears to recognize that effective solutions cannot be accomplished without substantial federal participation.

TABLE 20

PERCENTAGE FAVORING DECENTRALIZATION

(selected four or more items)

National	44
Democrat	42
Republican	47
Independent	47
Nixon: approve	45
disapprove	45
East	38
Midwest	44
South	46
West	40
College	52
High school	43
Grade school	36
18 to 29 years	42
30 to 49 years	39
50 years and over	49
$15,000 and over	47
$10,000–$14,999	49
$7,000–$9,999	40
$5,000–$6,999	40
$3,000–$4,999	44
Under $3,000	37
Professional and business	50
White collar	53
Manual worker	40
Farmer	31

These attitudes are not out of line with the operating realities of the federal system. The traditional rhetoric of federalism has stressed distinct functional divisions among national, state, and local levels (the layercake, so to speak), but the system has always turned out to be more like a marble cake, with an intermingling and sharing of functions. The respective levels of government are partners in a common enterprise; any doctrinaire position that fails to take this historical fact into account is, in the end, bound to be found wanting. This is no less true of President Nixon's outspoken condemnation of the federal effort than it is of Democrats who arbitrarily rule out new approaches that call for greater relative involvement by states and localities. At this point, the Democrats should focus more directly on the doctrinaire quality of the Nixon strategy and demonstrate how this approach, if implemented, would inevitably result in a critical diminution of certain governmental services that are clearly favored by a solid majority of the public.[21]

THE ISSUE OF RACIAL JUSTICE

One of the Democrats' most sensitive dilemmas arises from its long-standing advocacy of civil rights and equal opportunity. So long as race remained an issue relatively remote from most Americans, the Democratic Party was able both to champion racial justice and win presidential elections. Two strands of the Kennedy-Johnson era, however, came together in the mid-1960s to force a national reckoning with the plight of racial minority groups, blacks in particular, and to change civil rights from a proud commitment of the national Democratic Party to a weighty political burden.

First, comprehensive civil rights legislation finally passed after nearly two decades of effort in the halls of Congress and in the segregated schools, parks, lunch counters, and buses of the South and border states. With this legislation that brought down the walls of legally sanctioned segregation and discrimination came a new sense of hope and dignity among blacks—ever the poignant source of heightened expectations, frustrations, despair, and reaction.

The second strand grew out of the Great Society and its "war on poverty." For the first time, "the poor," as such, were singled out for special national attention, and significant commitments of national resources were approved by Congress. While the aims of these programs were in the best traditions of the Democratic Party, a number of difficult by-products soon emerged. With increased visibility, the poor acquired the public stigma of dependency upon the welfare and social services provided by the federal government, even though the programs were designed explicitly to break that dependency.

The increasingly outraged reaction of the nonpoor was not far behind. Walter Dean Burnham characterized this violation of the conventional political morality in his MIT memorandum:

> Politically created threats to my own economic well-being, and especially to the prospects of success for my children, are an intolerable usurpation, which interferes with the right order of things. This is particularly intolerable when, as a result of pressure-group activities and support from the bleeding-heart intellectual elites, I am expected to consent to this jeopardy for the sake of people who are unwilling or incompetent to "make it on their own" as I did.[22]

Although clearly not intended, tensions between the races were redefined and rechanneled into the issue of poverty and welfare.[23] No longer was it the simple characterization of racial bigot against integrationist. The issue became defined in broader political terms and provoked many persons not really affected up to then by the struggle for racial justice.

During these years poll findings evidenced the public's impatience with the pace of integration. In a Gallup sounding in March 1965, 34 per cent of the public felt that the Johnson Administration was "pushing integration too fast"; 55 per cent felt the pace was either not fast enough or about right. In June 1968, three years later, the question was repeated and 45 per cent felt things were moving "too fast" as against 44 per cent feeling the Johnson Administration was pushing integration "not fast enough" or "about right." The potency of the issue was also noted in the May 1972 survey discussed in

Chapter 1: 69 per cent agreed that "blacks and people in other minorities expect things to improve too quickly and are making unreasonable demands."

With the complex range of issues posed by Governor Wallace's candidacy in 1968 and 1972, the Democratic Party was forced into a corner—no better illustrated than by the terrible political dilemma posed by the busing issue. Can the party afford to retain its traditional advocacy of civil rights and political consequences be damned? Or must the party fudge the issue in hopes of forestalling even wider defections at the polls of those who subscribe to the conventional political morality as characterized by Burnham?

There is, of course, no easy or pat answer to either question. But in searching at least for an approach to the problem, if not a total solution, it is reasonable to make three assumptions: (1) The Democratic Party is not going to renege on its basic commitment to securing racial justice. (2) Public opposition to "civil rights," plus the changing nature of the problem itself, renders impracticable many of the approaches that the party followed in the 1950s and 1960s. (3) It is imperative that the party learn how to talk about racial matters in a way least provocative to those voters whose support is essential for building a majority presidential coalition in 1976— that is, to casual Democrats and independents.

The January 1973 Gallup survey assessed the impact of alternative formulations of ways to sustain forward movement on the racial front in the mid-1970s without suffering debilitating political losses. It is not surprising that the rationale found least acceptable was one based on the principle of quotas: "Because they have not been given a fair chance for so long, blacks and other minority groups should now be given special preference over others when it comes to things like jobs and being admitted into colleges and labor unions." Fully 80 per cent of those sampled disagreed with this line of argument, 15 per cent agreed, and 5 per cent had no opinion.

The classic integrationist formulation also met with resistance. A majority (52 per cent) disagreed with the proposition that "the only way to achieve true equality for blacks and other minority groups is for the federal government to keep pushing hard for integration in all aspects of American life." Forty-four percent agreed, 5 per cent had no opinion.

Spokesmen such as Vernon Jordan, executive director of the National Urban League, have attempted to distinguish between the imposition of rigid quotas and the necessity of affirmative action programs and compensatory initiatives by government. With such an approach in mind, the January 1973 survey included this statement: "To make up for what has happened in the past, the federal government should make a special effort to help blacks and other minority groups by spending more money for things like education, housing, and fighting the problem of crime and drugs." This formulation generated less opposition than either the quota or traditional integrationist position: 58 per cent agreed with it, 37 per cent disagreed, and 4 per cent had no opinion.

The most acceptable solution, however, proved to be this: "The only way the problems of blacks and other minority groups can be solved is for the federal government to make an all-out effort by spending much more money on domestic problems affecting all Americans, like health, education, housing, and improving things in our cities." With this statement nearly two-thirds (65 per cent) agreed. Twenty-seven per cent disagreed and 8 per cent had no opinion. More significantly, the high levels of support were sustained across the broad range of demographic groupings needed for a majority Democratic coalition. The divisions that plagued McGovern in 1972 disappeared.

The message from these data is unambiguous, at least in terms of measuring the political risks of a strategy based on quotas for blacks and other minorities as opposed to a strategy that seeks to attack black problems as part of a broader offensive against national domestic problems generally. Any political appeal that appears, rightly or wrongly, to *guarantee* a special break for blacks or other racial minorities, as such, is going to be difficult to sell to a majority of Americans. This is not to suggest, in any sense, a strategy of "benign neglect." But it is to say that if the Democratic Party hopes both to

carry forward the cause of racial justice, a struggle in which
President Nixon has evinced limited interest, *and* rebuild a
majority presidential coalition capable of governing the country, it must deal with problems of black Americans and other
minorities primarily in the context of problems faced by
many other nonblack Americans.

There is additional evidence that supports the validity of
this approach. Watts and Free found that blacks sensed just
about as much personal progress from past to present as
whites (although at a lower level of personal achievement)
and that blacks "were significantly *more* optimistic about their
personal futures." [24] In other words, if Watts and Free's finding is accurate, blacks and other minorities appear to have
reached a point where their future progress can be pursued
realistically as part of the larger nation without jeopardizing
either progress or stability. There appears to be no firm disposition among Americans to back away from national solutions to the specific problems that now comprise the "racial"
issue—education, housing, jobs, health care, drugs, and even
welfare. It seems likely, moreover, that the flammability of
the busing issue will continue slowly to decline as solutions are
arrived at locally and implemented with varying degrees of
success, and as the federal courts provide states and localities
with greater leeway to find compromise solutions. The national Democratic Party's position, set forth in the 1972 platform, that busing remains one of many available tools for
achieving quality education does not fly in the face of current operational realities. The issue remains difficult, to be
sure, but time, at last, seems to be working for a resolution of
the Democratic Party's dilemma on busing.

But there should be no illusion that the path to successful
handling of the racial issue will be easy to follow politically,
especially for any Democrat seeking the presidential nomination. It represents a departure from expected Democratic
rhetoric. Patience and diplomacy will be needed for any
approach like this to have a chance of working. But the evidence that the public is ready to support expanded governmental initiatives in major areas of black concern argues that

such a strategy holds out the best long-term hope for meaningful minority progress *and* political success for the party generally.

THE ECONOMIC AND SOCIAL ISSUES

No analysis of public attitudes about current problems of governing the United States would be complete without some attention to what Richard Scammon and Ben Wattenberg chose to identify as the nation's two major "voting issues." In their 1970 book, *The Real Majority*, Scammon and Wattenberg identified a voting issue as one that "continues to hold sway over the electorate for many consecutive years or even consecutive decades." [25] It has been clear since the days of FDR that the economy was such an issue. Historically, it has helped Democrats to win elections. But as the decade of the 1960s closed, Scammon and Wattenberg discovered an issue that helped the Republicans. They wrote:

> In the years until the election of 1968, the battlefield had been mostly an economic battlefield, and the Democrats held the ideological allegiance of the machinist and his wife from the suburbs of Dayton, and tens of millions other middle-income, middle-educated, middle-aged voters . . . That seems to be changing. For the seventies, the battlefield shows signs of splitting into two battle fields: the old economic one and the new social one that deals with crime, drugs, racial pressure and disruption.[26]

We have seen that in the congressional elections of 1970 the Democrats capitalized on the economic issue and more or less neutralized what Scammon and Wattenberg named "the Social Issue," despite the dedicated efforts of Spiro Agnew and Richard Nixon to make it otherwise. As a consequence, the Democrats did surprisingly well on Election Day. By 1972, however, George McGovern's pervasive lack of credibility with the voters and the failure of his campaign to exploit President Nixon's known vulnerabilities produced a very different result. Given these electoral developments since Scammon and Wattenberg made their observations, not to mention the

Watergate disclosures and the nation's most recent economic troubles, it seems necessary to look again at the place of the economic issue and the social issue in American politics. Do they still dominate the hearts and minds of voters? Will they be decisive factors for the Democrats as they strive for a comeback in 1974 and a successful presidential campaign in 1976?

Several observations seem to be in order. First, there is little doubt that inflation stands above all other issues in the public's mind as the nation's most important problem. Principal elements of the social issue—crime and drug abuse—are close behind. Another element—unrest or alienation in American life—appears to be on the wane. In May 1973 the Gallup Poll reported the most important problems facing the country today, as the table below indicates.

TABLE 21
Most Important Problem Facing the Country Today

Percentage selecting:

High cost of living	62
Crime and lawlessness	17
Drugs	16
Corruption in government/Watergate	16
Pollution	9
Unemployment	9
Race relations	8
Other international problems	8
Southeast Asia situation	7
World peace	6
Welfare	5
Poverty	5
Energy crisis	4
"Big government"	4
General unrest in nation	4
Other problems	25
No opinion	12

More recent data, such as the study conducted by Louis Harris and Associates, in September 1973 for the U.S. Senate Subcommittee on Intergovernmental Relations, confirm the sharp drop in the public's concern over the war in Indochina and the decline of race and discrimination and tax reform as major issues but show an extraordinary jump in "integrity in government" as an issue of concern, hardly a surprise in the year of Watergate and Operation Candor. In fact, Harris reports an increase of thirty-eight points between 1972 and 1973 in the percentage of persons selecting "integrity in government" as one of the country's two or three biggest problems, placing it second only to "economy/inflation."

The chairman of the subcommittee and its ranking Republican, Senators Edmund S. Muskie and Edward J. Gurney, jointly commented in a foreword to the study that, "for the first time in the 10 years of opinion sampling by the Harris Survey, the growing trend of public opinion toward disenchantment with government swept more than half of all Americans with it. . . . The discontent was not limited to the traditionally discontented: The elderly, Southerners, skilled laborers, and residents of rural communities all shared similar strong feelings of powerlessness and distress." But Muskie and Gurney went on to note that 90 per cent of Americans—and a like percentage of state and local officials—"are convinced that government can work effectively and well. Both share a faith in the ability of government, specifically the unpopular Federal establishment, to subordinate special influence to the general welfare and to bring in first-rate people whose first priorities will be 'helping the country' and 'caring about the people.' " [27] The implications of this finding for the Democratic Party will be developed more fully in chapters 5 and 6.

Most importantly, however, the Nixon Administration remained vulnerable on the economic issue, with negative public attitudes on price increases in mid-summer 1973 surpassing the levels of mid-1971 before President Nixon's announcement of his New Economic Policy.

The Harris Survey periodically asks the question: "Do you feel the prices of most things you buy are rising more rapidly than a year ago, about as rapidly as they were then, less rapidly than a year ago, or are they going down?" In July 1973, 90 per cent of those interviewed answered "more rapidly," up from 49 per cent in December 1972, 47 per cent in December 1971, and 73 per cent in March 1971. This increase of 41 percentage points between December 1972 and July 1973 of those who felt prices were rising "more rapidly" than a year earlier was the steepest rise in this category since Nixon became President. It wiped out the gains that he had achieved on the economic front at the conclusion of his first term, when, as both Harris and Gallup reported, the economic outlook of Americans was brighter and more optimistic than at any time since Nixon took office.

A comparable, although not quite as drastic, picture emerges of the public's attitude on the question of economic recession. In response to the question, "By this time next year, do you think the country will be in a recession or not?" the Harris Survey in July 1973 (see Table 22) reported a steep rise in the percentage of those who foresaw a recession in 1974.

TABLE 22
WILL THE COUNTRY BE IN A RECESSION BY THIS TIME NEXT YEAR?

	percentage answering:		
	Will	Will Not	Not Sure
July 1973	46	26	28
December 1972	26	43	31
September 1972	22	44	34
November 1970	48	25	27

In other words, after four phases of economic controls, a landslide re-election victory, and evidence of solid progress in building the public's confidence on his handling of economic issues, President Nixon in mid-summer 1973 was back to where he stood in late 1970 and early 1971, or worse, at least as far as the public's view of his economic policies was concerned. Inflation was rampant and fears of a recession were rising.

This regression on the economic front seemed particularly serious for President Nixon and the Republicans since it coincided with and reinforced the public's traditional general perception that the country fares better economically under Democrats. Even the McGovern candidacy did not totally erase the Democratic advantage in this area, according to Gallup Organization data (see Table 22).

Unless the economy improves dramatically over the course of the next two years, the Republican presidential candidate

TABLE 23

WHICH PARTY WILL DO A BETTER JOB
OF KEEPING THE COUNTRY PROSPEROUS?

percentage answering:

	Democrats	GOP	No Difference
October 1966	39	24	37
June 1970	44	29	27
July 1971	46	23	21
August 1972	38	35	27

in 1976 is likely to find himself saddled with a heavy political burden in terms of the economic issue.

On the issues of crime or lawlessness, drugs, racial pressure, and social disruption—the cutting edges of the social issue— the Democrats, while potentially vulnerable, are in a stronger position than they were four years ago in the wake of the 1968 campaign. As disclosed by both Louis Harris and the Gallup Poll, crime/lawlessness and drugs are at or near the top of the public's list of major national problems, even after four years of the Nixon Presidency that assigned them priority attention. Watts and Free also report almost no sense of national progress in combating crime in the twelve months prior to June 1972. Indeed, 51 per cent believed the nation had either lost some or lost much ground in 1971–72. (See Table 24.) A slightly better picture emerged on the issue of drug abuse, although great room for improvement remains.[28]

TABLE 24

AMOUNT OF PROGRESS, JULY 1971–JUNE 1972

percentage answering:

	Crime	Drugs
Made much progress	1	3
Made some progress	19	31
Stood still	26	21
Lost some ground	32	23
Lost much ground	19	18
Don't know	3	4

The fantastic economic and political events of 1973, in combination with the Nixon· Administration's longer-term record, appear to have given the Democratic Party a significant advantage in terms of the economic issue and largely neutralized the party's real or potential vulnerability on the social issue, assuming some minimum level of political common sense among the Democrats. The President asked for, and received, broad discretion from Congress in handling the nation's economy. His offensive against congressional Democrats on the spending issue petered out as Watergate unfolded, and as Congress agreed to work within the President's total spending limit while reserving the right to reshuffle priorities. Even if highly volatile food prices should respond to the Republicans' frantic efforts to expand the supply of basic commodities, the burden of economic performance is squarely on the Nixon Administration and the accumulated damage of the past five years is considerable. Two other factors should be kept in mind:

- The public clearly favors strict wage-price controls, but, as noted in Chapter 1, people tend to see the application of wage-price controls by the Nixon Administration as unfair, favoring business and financial institutions at the expense of wage earners.
- This attitude reflects, at least in part, the view among many Americans that President Nixon and the Republican Party in general are "too close to big business"; or, to express the same attitude another way, a large majority of Americans (77 per cent as reported by Harris in February 1973) believe that the Nixon Administration should be tougher on big business in the second term than it was in the first.

To sum up: As the voters make their retrospective judgments in 1974 and 1976, the Democrats should find the Nixon economic record working in their favor and should have no reason to be on the defensive on the social issue, if only because it will be nearly impossible for the Republicans to take the offensive.

From all of this emerges a picture that is less confusing than might initially seem. Principally, I believe, because of sensitive political antennae and a personal understanding of their constituents (plus the chance to duck some of the more difficult national issues), Democrats in the states and in Congress have responded more effectively than the national party to the "deepest transitional crisis in [American] history" that Burnham has described. Consequently, a Democratic majority survives below the presidential level. But as the party strives to enlarge this congressional majority in future presidential elections, it should focus on three conclusions that emerge from these data:

1. If one accepts V. O. Key's dictum that voters judge retrospectively, then Republican troubles in handling the economy and their neutralizing of the social issue have given the Democrats elbow room to direct their energies to demonstrating a renewed concern for the interests of individual citizens in terms of their daily problems, together with proving that government still has the capacity to deal *competently* and *fairly* with these human concerns.

2. Whether the issue is government spending, the decentralization of government power, or the knotty problem of racial justice, there is a popular longing for more than rigid and doctrinaire approaches that, by their very nature, appear to submerge the perceived needs of people, or that clash with the electorate's ingrained ideological conservatism.

3. But there also exists a refreshing, even surprising, willingness on the part of the American people to support governmental intervention in a host of domestic problem areas so long as this involvement is understandable in their own terms and is seen as basically fair to all.

Thus it would be a grave mistake to assume that the passing of the New Deal ideology necessarily heralds an era of government unconcern for the human problems that have been such a prominent feature of Democratic agendas for the past forty years. This would represent the most serious misreading of current public attitudes. As a consequence, the Democratic

Party's dilemma of "liberalism" may, in fact, be an artificial dilemma that can be resolved without the internecine strife that has highlighted internal Democratic politics in recent years. The answer seems to lie in focusing on new and more productive ways to use the federal government's considerable power in solving current domestic problems and in building the political institutions that can insure the more responsive and creative application of this power at all levels of American society.

5

COALITION
AND IDEOLOGY:
PERSPECTIVE
OF THE '70s

As the mid-term elections in 1974 and the presidential elections of 1976 draw closer, the Democratic Party is faced with an unusual—indeed a rather astonishing—mixture of political advantages and problems. Whether Democrats can capitalize on the advantages and at least begin solving the problems will determine how the party does in these elections and in elections for the next ten years.

The next two years—1974 and 1975—present what may be one last chance for the Democratic Party. Some reasons:

1. Despite the dimensions of the Nixon landslide, the President was not given a clear-cut "mandate" by the voters in the sense that they specifically endorsed his position on a number of domestic issues. Watergate, moreover, made hash of any mandate in operational terms. The President's 1972-73 winter offensive against the Democratic Congress on the question of federal spending, closely linked to his concept of the New Federalism, "returning power to the people," bogged down as Watergate gained momentum during the spring and summer of 1973. The Democrats, in other words, were handed an unexpected chance to regroup and rethink their counter-strategy.

2. President Nixon's mishandling of the economy, together with such other items as gasoline and fuel oil shortages, the financial irregularities associated with his San Clemente and

Key Biscayne homes, the resignation of Vice President Agnew, and the difficulties in implementing the New Federalism at the state and local levels provided the Democrats with a package of highly visible, highly volatile, deeply felt political issues. If, as V. O. Key suggests, the electorate judges retrospectively, the Democrats now appear to be sitting pretty.

3. The New Deal coalition pieced together by Franklin D. Roosevelt survives at the congressional level, even though there have been serious defections in the past two presidential elections, and provides a base on which the Democratic Party can begin building a presidential majority.

The Democrats, however, appear not at all certain how to handle these political assets. For example, considerable ambivalence has been displayed by Democratic spokesmen in dealing with the Watergate disclosures. The more vigorous assertion of congressional power on selected issues has not resulted in a coherent legislative strategy that could be viewed as a Democratic program. This uncertainty can be explained, in large part, by the party's lack of clarity about its own role and purpose in contemporary American society. The demise of the New Deal ideology and the abortive appeal of the New Politics have left the party confused and unsure of how best to exploit the political riches that President Nixon has left on the Democratic doorstep.

Chapter 4 examined public attitudes on five major questions—government spending, decentralization of federal power, racial justice, the economy, and the social issue—in an effort to begin defining what a new and more coherent Democratic appeal to the electorate might comprise. Not surprisingly, as long as a well-defined link is forged between governmental activity and the needs of individual citizens, as in the successful congressional and state races of 1972, the voters display more pragmatism and flexibility on these questions than much of the contemporary political rhetoric would lead one to expect.

This chapter will attempt to translate general voter attitudes into tactical suggestions for the evolution of a Democratic ideology for 1974–76—and beyond. That the process has to be seen as evolutionary—largely one of trial and error—should come as no surprise, given the nondoctrinaire nature of American politics and the traditional aversion of American parties to a highly specific and definitive ideology. What is alarming is that the party today lacks the sense of direction and basic ideas to initiate such a process.

If the voters judge retrospectively, they also, according to Key, "respond to what they see and hear." Much of the Democratic problem of the present and the recent past is tied to a perplexity about what the electorate should see and hear from the Democratic side of the aisle (or street, depending on one's locus of operations). This uncertainty is abetted by a lack of clarity on another important question: Who, in the mid-1970s, *are* the Democrats?

THE DEMOCRATIC CONSTITUENCY

In addition to helping elect and re-elect Richard Nixon, the defection of key elements of the New Deal coalition in 1968 and 1972 produced a troublesome identity crisis for the national Democratic Party. It was a jolting realization that partisan stalwarts of the Roosevelt era, such as urban Catholics or blue-collar workers, could no longer be counted on in the contest for the Presidency. As a consequence, a number of pet theories on the best way to rebuild a majority presidential coalition quickly surfaced.

The "ethnics," for example, were deemed to be crucial. Or corralling new voters. Or launching a counteroffensive to Mr. Nixon's "Catholic strategy." Or luring blue-collar voters away from the siren songs of Governor Wallace and the President. In many cases, Democratic theorists were primarily reflecting their own personal political associations or biases; little attention was paid to the changing nature of the American electorate or to the relationship of the Democratic Party to these changes. Thus, prescriptions for regaining the party's political health generally have been cast in terms that reflected the realities of another generation, with only occasional links to the world of the mid-1970s.

One way to regain some badly needed perspective on the

composition of the current Democratic constituency is to cal-
culate its demographic profile—that is, to look at a dimension,
like age, and determine the percentage of all Democratic
voters found in each age category. For example, in a Gallup
Poll taken in the fall of 1972, 49 per cent of those under
twenty-five years of age preferred McGovern over Nixon. This
represented McGovern's strongest showing among all age
groups. Such a finding was cited by some persons to support
the proposition that the youth vote was pivotal to the Senator's
campaign. But the full demographic profile reveals that only
12 per cent of the nation's Democratic voters were under
twenty-five years of age—a discovery that might have given
pause to those caught up in the mythology that young voters,
per se, held the key to winning elections in the early 1970s.

At the outset, the advantages and limitations to this approach should be made clear. First, as to the limitations: It
is doubtful that a person's demographic characteristics (for
example, age, income level, education, place of residence,
etc.) are necessarily the key to his voting behavior in any
given election, except as the issues or choice of candidates in
the election relate directly to specific attributes or interests of
that demographic group. If, for example, right-to-work laws
were visibly at issue, it could be assumed that most labor
union members would vote *as* labor union members in that
election. Otherwise, the individual's voting decision is likely
to reflect a complicated web of concerns and interests, not all
of which can be captured in demographic terms.

The division of each demographic dimension—age, educational level, income level, etc.—by percentage might also imply
a static quality to the electorate that would be misleading. In
fact, the constituency of a national party is constantly in
motion, as millions of voters switch allegiances in any election
or join the ranks of the nonvoters, just as millions of new
voters enter the arena and past dropouts decide to participate.
Finally, this demographic profile is not a precise blueprint
like those used in an effort to capture the electoral votes
that decide presidential elections. Such an analysis requires
an evaluation of the political conditions peculiar to each state,

as well as the demographic and electoral characteristics of that state.

But these limitations are not sufficient to do away with one considerable advantage, especially at this point in Democratic Party history. The demographic profile provides, at one glance, a portrait of "Democratic voters" in their totality and in a manner that illuminates significant demographic relationships within the Democratic constituency that otherwise might be missed. Admittedly, the portrait is drawn with broad strokes and is one that will continue to change. But it also turns out to be a portrait of Democratic voters very different from many traditional assumptions about who are the Democrats.

Registered voters who indicated in a September 1972 Gallup Poll a preference for the Democratic candidate in their local congressional race provide the base for this demographic profile. These persons are labeled "Democratic voters" on the assumption that their electoral dispositions were more indicative of a functional majority than either those who simply called themselves "Democrats" or those who leaned toward McGovern. In fact, Gallup reported in this poll that 50 per cent declared their intention to vote Democratic in the congressional race, as contrasted to 43 per cent calling themselves "Democrats" and 32 per cent favoring McGovern over Nixon. The "defection rate" for each population group—that is, the percentage of "Democratic voters" (as defined above) who did not intend to vote for McGovern—is also calculated.

Table 25 (below) shows that eight of every ten Democratic voters (82 per cent) are "over thirty" and four of every ten (42 per cent) are over fifty years of age. Almost half (49 per cent) of Democratic voters between thirty and fifty defected from McGovern, as did more than one-third (37 per cent) of those over fifty. In other words, the highest defection rates took place among the age categories that contained the highest percentages of Democratic voters.

Table 26 shows that three-fourths (74 per cent) of Democratic voters today have acquired *more* than a grade-school education, a direct consequence of the upward mobility of

TABLE 25

	Per Cent of Democratic Voters	Per Cent Defecting
18 to 24 years	12	5
25 to 29 years	7	20
30 to 49 years	39	49
50 years and over	42	37
	100	

Americans since the New Deal. The highest defection rate (42 per cent) occurred among Democratic voters with some high school, but no college, education. Again, this was the category with the highest percentage of Democratic voters.

TABLE 26

	Per Cent of Democratic Voters	Per Cent Defecting
College	23	33
High school	51	42
Grade school	26	29
	100	

Table 27 shows that fully half (51 per cent) of Democratic voters live in a household whose income falls in the upper and upper-middle brackets, i.e., over $10,000 annually. Persons earning less than $5,000 a year comprise less than one-fourth (23 per cent) of Democratic voters. The conventional dichotomy between affluent Republicans and impecunious Democrats is apparently due for some revision. Those Democrats most opposed to McGovern were found in the middle-income bracket—between $7,000 and $10,000 annually—with a defection rate of 47 per cent.

Table 28 shows that the largest single group of Democratic voters is found among those categorized as professional and business (27 per cent). This deviation from traditional assumptions about the pivotal role of workers in the Democratic constituency is lessened by combining skilled workers (16 per cent) and unskilled workers (23 per cent) for a total

TABLE 27

	Per Cent of Democratic Voters	Per Cent Defecting
$15,000 and over	22	40
$10,000–$14,999	29	42
$7,000–$9,999	14	47
$5,000–$6,999	12	26
$3,000–$4,999	10	31
Under $3,000	13	27
	100	

of 39 per cent. The nonlabor force, mostly retired persons, is one-fifth (20 per cent) of the total. Farmers comprise but 5 per cent. The most serious defections took place among skilled workers—fully one-half abandoned McGovern's candidacy.

TABLE 28

	Per Cent of Democratic Voters	Per Cent Defecting
Professional and business	27	39
White collar	9	33
Skilled workers	16	51
Unskilled workers	23	37
Farmers	5	54
Nonlabor force	20	24
	100	

Nearly three-quarters (73 per cent) of Democratic voters live in the East, Midwest, and West, and the defection rates in these regions were lower than in the Deep South and Border States—where more than one-half of Democratic voters left McGovern. These figures support the notion that the party's traditional problem of reconciling political demands of the South and non-South has been displaced by the need to cope with new tensions between the established Democratic majorities in the Northeastern states and the emerging majorities in the Upper Midwest and the West Coast.[1]

The Deep South provides but 8 per cent of Democratic voters. (See Table 29.) It should be noted, however, that over one-half of those living in the South leaned Democratic at the congressional level and that Democratic moderates have done well in recent years in gubernatorial races. Although the Deep South remains a source of continuing trouble for the Democrats in presidential elections, it is obvious that the party cannot afford simply to write off the 130 electoral votes contained in the Deep South.

TABLE 29

	Per Cent of Democratic Voters	Per Cent Defecting
East	30	26
Midwest	26	33
Deep South	8	53
Border	19	54
West	17	34
	100	

Protestants comprise more than one-half (52 per cent) of Democratic voters; Catholics less than one-third (32 per cent); and Jews 5 per cent. Given the attention paid to Catholic defections in 1972, it is noteworthy that (as Table 30 shows) Protestant defections were higher (41 per cent compared to 36 per cent). These national totals, however, do not contradict the observation that the major reason for the dropoff in McGovern's support in the Northeast, compared to Humphrey's in 1968, can be largely explained by a massive shift to Nixon by Roman Catholic voters.[2]

TABLE 30

	Per Cent of Democratic Voters	Per Cent Defecting
Protestant	52	41
Catholic	32	36
Jewish	5	*
Other	11	*
	100	

* Too few cases for statistically meaningful percentages.

Nearly two-thirds (63 per cent) of all Democratic voters live in localities where the population is *less* than half a million persons. (See Table 31.) One-fourth (25 per cent) are found in cities of 1 million and over. McGovern lost heavily in smaller cities and suburban areas where the defection rates were 36 per cent, compared to 28 per cent in cities of one million and over. In rural areas (which provide 22 per cent of Democratic voters), the defection rate shot up to 47 per cent.

Finally, the percentage distribution between white and nonwhite Democrats holds no surprises: 81 per cent of Democratic voters are white; 19 per cent are nonwhite. (See Table 32.) Nonwhites, however, produced one of the lower defection rates—18 per cent—compared to the 42 per cent rate for white Democrats.

TABLE 31

	Per Cent of Democratic Voters	Per Cent Defecting
1 million and over	25	28
500,000–999,999	12	36
50,000–499,999	30	36
2,500–49,999	11	37
Under 2,500	22	47
	100	

TABLE 32

	Per Cent of Democratic Voters	Per Cent Defecting
White	81	42
Nonwhite	19	18
	100	

Two principal conclusions result from this analysis. First of all, it is clear that the Democratic Party must reach beyond the boundaries of the traditional New Deal coalition if its full electoral potential is to be realized. That is, *although the FDR coalition held together at the congressional level in 1972, despite McGovern's poor showing, it provides only a portion of the base on which Democrats must build in the 1976 presidential campaign.*

To focus on the grade-school-educated, for example, ignores 74 per cent of Democratic voters. To appeal to the blue-collar workers (skilled and unskilled) overlooks the remaining 61 per cent of the Democrats. Similarly, to concentrate on persons near the bottom of the socio-economic pyramid (such as households with a yearly income under $7,000) leaves out 65 per cent of Democratic voters.

A special computation by the Gallup Organization for this book disclosed that blue-collar workers, grade-school-educated, persons in households with a yearly income under $7,000, Catholics, and nonwhites—the core of the New Deal coalition —accounted for only 38 per cent of the "Democratic voters" in the fall of 1972. The remaining 62 per cent comprised the high school- and college-educated, persons of higher income, business and professional persons, Protestants, residents of smaller cities, and the like.

Second, the demographic profile of Democratic voters supports the thesis developed in the last chapter: that *the party's future cannot be seen as a choice between the advocates of the New Politics—appealing to the poor, the blacks, the young, and intellectuals—or those who counsel a return to the familiar demography of the New Deal.* The constituency that is potentially available to the Democrats in the 1970s is broader and more diverse than many persons imagined. The party must not permit its attention, or its ideology, to be restricted by formulations that reflect political circumstances very different from those existing today.

The breadth and heterogeneity of the Democratic coalition further suggest the danger of relying upon highly specialized appeals to discrete segments of the electorate in presidential campaigns. Although such specialized appeals may work politically in certain local situations, it is not sufficient, clearly, for the national Democratic Party to base a presidential campaign on rhetorical appeals that isolate, for example, labor union members, or Catholics, or those with less than a high school education. The evolution of a *de facto* quota system in the selection of Democratic National Convention delegates

—a system that gave special standing to women, young people, and minorities—provided a striking illustration of the limits and dangers of such a strategy.

In this sense, then, the era of "interest-group liberalism" is over for the Democrats. Of course, the party cannot win without substantial elements of the traditional New Deal coalition, but neither can it win unless it moves beyond the coalition's boundaries. This, in turn, suggests the wisdom of searching for concerns that are common to this broad spectrum of Americans who can be identified as "Democratic voters." Or, to put the issue another way: *Who* the party talks to is perhaps less important than *how* the party talks and acts. It is imperative that the Democratic Party recognize the importance of thinking about, talking about, and acting on the increasingly interrelated, inseparable worlds of politicking and governing.

THE DEMOCRATIC PERSPECTIVE

Since the days of the New Deal, the public has looked to the federal government—the major institution of American society committed to the economic well-being of the American people—as the principal guardian of the opportunity for upward mobility. The chance for one's children to surpass the economic and social accomplishments of their parents has long been a distinguishing feature of American life and a vital element of our conventional political morality. This recognition of the federal government's role, however, did not diminish the public's acceptance of a value system that glorified individual initiative, free enterprise, and hard work as necessary ingredients in the struggle to get ahead. Despite the increasing scope of federal activity, the belief has persisted that people get pretty much what they deserve, that hard work and dedication still pay off.

With the passage of time, most American families have come into an affluence that is new, not that their lives have reached a plateau of abundance that is fully satisfying, but that many elements traditionally associated with the American Dream of material well-being have been fulfilled. As a con-

sequence of this feeling of personal progress, a solid majority
of Americans now looks to the federal government less as a
protector of the opportunities for personal advancement and
more as a protector of the economic and social gains those
opportunities have made possible.[3]

This perception of the federal government as protector of
economic and social gains becomes even more pronounced in
these days of high inflation. Whether it expresses itself in
staunch opposition to higher taxes or in substantial agreement
with the conservative ideology that condemns government
"spending," the attitude that favors federal restraint in
domestic activities—at least at the level of general discussion—
looms large in any assessment of the contemporary political
scene.

If this were the sum of the public's attitudes, President
Nixon's studied appeal to the "New American Majority"
would be just about invulnerable politically. But as Watts
and Free discovered in polling for *State of the Nation*, many
Americans, despite their realization of the American Dream,
"have experienced disillusionment and even ennui. . . . Even
with a second car, a freezer of TV dinners, and an electric
toothbrush, Americans seem to be saying, 'Is this all we can
look forward to from now on?' " [4] Then, of course, there are
the Americans who have a long way to go before a second car
becomes a problem—the 25 million who fall below what the
government now calls the "low income level" and the millions more who barely survive from paycheck to paycheck.

Watts and Free also discerned that the public's attention has
shifted dramatically from international problems to a broad
range of domestic issues: "Every single item on the domestic
side . . . registered higher in the public's scheme of spending
priorities than national defense and any of the purely international items." [5] They characterized the current American
attitude toward the "state of the nation" with these words:

We are doing well enough in our own personal lives. The country
has made some progress too, both domestically and internationally,
over the past year. It is up from the rock-bottom low it hit in

1971. But, despite this improvement, the state of the nation is just "fair to middling." As a country we still have a long way to go, and to get there we will have to make some basic changes in the way we govern ourselves.[6]

These attitudes, moreover, existed fully a year before the Watergate case broke open and the full surge of Phase III inflation, together with food and fuel shortages, gripped the country.

The Nixon Administration's wholesale assault on the role of the federal government—launched in the early months of 1973 —is not likely to provide the answers for which the American people are ultimately searching, even though much of the Nixonian rhetoric coincides with the country's conventional political morality. It is not enough simply to protect the gains of a society that is viewed as only " fair-to-middling" by most of the people and that is seen as downright bad by some even lower on the socio-economic scale. But, by the same token, it is not likely that the Democratic Party can respond effectively to these troubled public attitudes about the state of the nation if its offering boils down to a choice between the interest-group liberalism of the New Deal or the counterculture of the New Politics.

One must begin, however, with the essential negativism of the Nixon alternative to the Democratic policies of the past generation. Since the days of the New Deal, the Republican Party has spent most of its creative energies, so to speak, criticizing the programmatic initiatives of the Democratic Party. Much of this, obviously, is due to the historical fact that Democrats have been in power for the greater portion of the post-Depression era. But the roots of Republican negativism run deeper and have their theoretical base. William F. Buckley, whose ideological facility must not be confused with frivolity, expresses a basic tenet of conservatism in his *Up from Liberalism*: namely, that it is fully appropriate and legitimate for the conservative to attack the activist propensities of the liberal without assuming the burden of suggesting what instead should be done. He writes:

A proposal that an end be put to the problem of poverty by as-
signing the task of eliminating it, plus three billion dollars per
year, to Mr. Sargent Shriver, does not require of the opposition a
careful catalogue of better uses to which three billion dollars
might be put. The "problem" of the conservative is less a philosophical problem, less—even—a practical problem, because the
mere defeat of a particular liberal proposal can have a highly
practical effect in forwarding a solution to the targeted problem
by conservative means.[7]

Despite the explicit lack of enthusiasm among the Buckley
clan for Nixon's candidacy in 1972 (not implying for a moment, of course, any affirmative feelings by the Buckleys for
President Nixon's opponent), the President and his advisers
clearly were following the broad outlines of what might be
called Buckley's strategy of "creative negativism." Alice M.
Rivlin of the Brookings Institution points out, in an analysis
of the Nixon budget reductions for 1974:

These cuts would not seem so disastrous if the President had
offered to replace them with superior programs. Even the small
positive social initiatives of his first term—welfare reform, health
insurance—have disappeared from this budget. The new budget
has lots of negatives but no positives.[8]

Rivlin notes that Nixon exacted disproportionate cuts in
the domestic budget because of his decision not to cut back
on national defense expenditures or to seek alternative revenue
sources through tax reform. He reduced or eliminated a
variety of social programs designed to help the poor, including housing, manpower training, emergency employment, and
legal services, without proposing any meaningful alternatives.
The concept of special revenue-sharing swallowed up other
Democratic programs, such as Model Cities and the Job
Corps, despite or, more probably, with the certain knowledge
that state and local governments would be hard put to find
the necessary monies to keep them alive. The Office of Economic Opportunity (OEO) was being dismantled.

Moreover, a closer reading of the fine print in the legislation proposed to implement special revenue sharing disclosed, for example, that many cities would suffer a loss of funds under the terms of the Better Communities Act that combined seven major urban development programs into a single noncategorical package. The nation's mayors responded by opposing the entire program until these defects were remedied. In a similar way, state and local officials have voiced grave misgivings over the operations of general revenue sharing. Instead of providing states and localities with extra money, it is having to fill the gaps left by the Administration's planned cutbacks in a host of domestic programs. The federal courts have jumped into the fray and declared that the President lacked the constitutional authority to abandon federal activities, like housing programs or road construction, without congressional approval, or to abolish by executive fiat legislatively created federal offices like OEO.

In terms of the earlier analysis of the public's ambivalence toward the role of the federal government, President Nixon managed to reap the benefits of both worlds during his first term: He talked like an ideological conservative but continued the federal government's traditional posture of operational liberalism, thus avoiding the trap into which Senator Goldwater stumbled in the 1964 campaign. As his second term began, however, the President began talking *and* acting like a conservative. If the findings in Chapter 4 are at all accurate, this shift should presage serious political difficulties as the effects of his newly found operational conservatism begin to take effect. By midsummer of 1973, the signs of rebellion were clearly visible in Congress, among the states and cities, and through a series of reverses in the federal courts. Over all these difficulties hung the gathering storm clouds of the nation's faltering economy and the growing sense that the Nixon Administration lacked the ability to find workable economic solutions.

This process of governmental paralysis and ineptitude is directly related to the value vacuum that envelopes so many facets of the Nixon Administration. The continuing drama of Watergate, the imaginative—if not to say illegal—methods for raising campaign funds, the ITT arrangement, the milk and wheat deals, the San Clemente and Key Biscayne homes, along with scores of other less-publicized indiscretions, are bound, over time, to heighten public unease over the apparent absence of a value base in the conduct of the Nixon Presidency. This, in turn, affects the vital ingredient of personal trust that is such a decisive factor—in this era of growing cynicism and alienation—in the public's evaluation of politicians and in the capacity of public officials to govern. As we saw in Chapter 3, underdog Democrat congressional campaigners succeeded in building a bond of personal trust with the voters by *acting* in a way that made them appear worthy of trust, not by *talking* about how trustworthy they really were.

The Nixon Administration throughout the summer and autumn of 1973 displayed an incredible insensitivity to these factors, especially in its handling of the Watergate case. The initial response was almost totally verbal—asserting over and over that White House and other highly placed Nixon officials were not involved. When events and continuing disclosures forced these denials to assume an "inoperative" status, the President still relied primarily on a strategy of hard-line rhetoric. Whatever the ultimate result of this extraordinary chapter in American political history, this much can be said: Whether presidential *actions* worthy of trust replace presidential *assertions* of trust in the coming months will have a major impact on Nixon's capacity to govern in his second term and, therefore, on the probable results of the 1974 and 1976 elections.

If the Democratic Party faces a crisis of legitimacy in the sense that neither the New Deal nor the New Politics offers an adequate ideological response to America's contemporary problems, so, too, does Nixon face a crisis of legitimacy even beyond the Watergate threat. His appeal to the "New American Majority" failed to take into account a whole range of real and perceived needs of the people who necessarily comprise that majority. It almost seems that President Nixon's response to the rising popular cynicism toward government, and the public's concurrent alienation from democratic institutions, is simply to join in the indictment.

But time has a way of getting things back in perspective. What happens when the jobs are not found, the welfare rolls continue to grow, the medical care is found wanting, the parks are not developed, and the low and moderate income housing is not built? Or, to put it another way, is the appeal of ideological conservatism sufficiently powerful to maintain public acceptance of its consequences? And at what point will the public's yearning for some higher purpose in our national life, as described by Watts and Free, reassert itself with a general housecleaning of Republican opportunists?

It can be argued that the Administration's disastrous domestic record since the President's second inaugural—in combination with the Watergate disclosures—has triggered these public reactions earlier than most persons would have predicted. But the basic question remains: What can the Democrats offer in this period of profound public disillusionment?

RETHINKING THE DEMOCRATIC CREDO

It is fewer years ago than it seems that President John F. Kennedy launched the nation on a very different course, one described by Kennedy critic Henry Fairlie in his book *The Kennedy Promise: The Politics of Expectation.* Fairlie writes:

> The arousal of an elevated sense of national purpose and the activity of the Presidency which accompanies it create what I call the politics of expectation. The people are encouraged to expect too much of their political institutions and of their political leaders. They cease to inquire what politics may accomplish for them, and what they must do for themselves. Instead, they expect politics to take the place which religion once held in their lives; and the politicians to be, not just archbishops . . . but cardinals; not just cardinals, but popes; not just popes, but saviors.[9]

One need not agree with the totality of Fairlie's argument— that the politics of expectation leads inexorably to the politics of crisis and the politics of confrontation—to recognize the hard-nosed common sense of the valedictory to the Democratic Party of President Kennedy's most valued and trusted political lieutenant, Lawrence F. O'Brien. In a totally unconscious, yet nonetheless explicit, repudiation of the politics of expectation, the departing Democratic National Chairman sounded a very different theme in his opening speech to the 1972 Democratic National Convention:

> An excessive pride in the past, coupled with future promises that few people believe, brought our Party—along with other institutions—to the present crisis of truth. . . . I think it comes down to this: Do we have the guts to level with the American people? . . . How do we level? We begin, I believe, with a few simple steps: we cool the excessive political rhetoric. We lighten the purple prose. We do not promise what we know cannot be delivered by man, God or the Democratic Party. . . .
>
> Now, we must stop kidding the American people. We must tell them the truth. I recognize, of course, that this idea runs counter to the whole history of American political talk. . . .
>
> Some will say that Americans are tired of making sacrifices. I say the American people are better than that. I say they will make the sacrifices if they can see the *sense* of the sacrifice. And when we level with them, that is *exactly* what we show them. . . . By being honest, direct and realistic, you have a chance to consciously break the vicious cycle of overpromising and underproducing that has corrupted us all.

In a very real sense, O'Brien's words particularize the meaning of the data examined in Chapter 4. "The American people . . . will make the sacrifice if they can see the *sense* of the sacrifice." Across a broad spectrum of governmental activities, the electorate is prepared to support a continuing, or greater, federal effort. There is little inclination among Americans simply to dump the most difficult and intractable domestic problems on the states and localities. There is a very substantial base among the public for continuing the fight against racial inequality as long as it is waged as part of a more comprehensive attack on the nation's economic and social problems.

Forthright and unapologetic criticism of its own past, coupled with a realistic agenda of more effective answers not solely dependent upon direct federal activism, can give the Democratic Party a base from which to think creatively once again about how best to solve the contemporary problems that restrict the lives and happiness of Americans. Unlike many Republicans, Democrats tend not to fear or dislike government, nor do they generally recoil from the frank expression of public attitudes. What is needed today among Democrats is a new perspective that liberates their inventiveness and their enthusiasm for the often untidy business of making government work.

The word "liberalism" either should be dropped from the Democratic lexicon or separated from the notion of direct federal activism. The commitment of the Democratic Party is to solving pressing problems—not to keeping the bureaucratic world of Washington busy. This, in turn, demands that the Democratic Party begin to think through alternative uses of the power that resides in the federal government. It cannot simply be a question of laying on more resources, services, and professionalism since the classic programmatic approach of the Great Society is no longer functional.[10] This is not meant to suggest, as President Nixon often does, that a great deal was not accomplished in President Johnson's years in terms of incomes raised, schools built, salaries of teachers improved, health centers established, Head Start classes organized, and so on down the line. But this judgment does reflect the growing consensus that the bureaucratic burden in Washington has become extremely heavy and that new ways have to be developed to simplify and rationalize the federal government's role in helping lesser units of government, and the private sector, attack the remaining problems.

It may well be possible that the federal government does not have to solve many of the problems itself; rather, the federal government's role, at least in part, can become one of ensuring that the problems *are* solved. Approached from this perspective, a number of alternative uses of federal power come to mind. It is not the purpose of this book to develop these functions in detail. However, the following strategies, which are in consonance with the propositions developed in the previous two chapters, deserve at least to be listed:

—A mixture of sanctions and rewards to force government bureaucracy—federal, state, and local—to respond directly to the needs and interests of individual citizens in terms they can understand and appreciate. If a citizen falls down in meeting his obligations to government, the citizen pays a penalty. If government defaults in meeting a commitment to citizens, the same thing should happen. The Internal Revenue Service, for example, might be required to pay 6 per cent interest on all personal income tax refunds that are not processed within thirty days of the citizen's filing his tax return. The financial compensation of victims of crime is another excellent illustration of this approach. Or, as Michael Novak has suggested, a system of financial rewards should be created for localities that agree to assume some of the more difficult and controversial social programs, such as scattersite housing, open housing, and school integration. Rather than having to resort to court orders to achieve these necessary steps, might it not be possible in some cases to provide the kind of financial incentives that encourage both voluntary compliance and stable, well-run communities? [11]

—Creative use of the federal tax code to foster social, as well as economic, objectives. It is a well-accepted principle that accelerated depreciation of capital goods and equipment is one way to increase the productive capacity of American industry. It is just as feasible to stimulate the private sector—corporations, foundations, voluntary associations, and the like—to make a more ambitious effort in taking on a variety of domestic problems that are handled less well by government bureaucracies.[12] There is, for example, a great need to explore ways of preserving the uniqueness of neighborhoods, particularly ethnic neighborhoods, to strengthen family ties and to bring the worlds of work and home more closely together. How can the economic and social forces that now contribute to a fragmenting of these basic human relationships be channeled in ways that result in a more personally satisfying occupational and living environment for millions of Americans who see their lives as only "fair-to-middling"? History has demonstrated the limited effect that government itself can have on these kinds of problems. But does that mean government is unable to help others who might do a more effective job?

—The enforcement of precise federal criteria and standards regarding the problem-solving activities that devolve to state and local governments, with particular attention to ensuring access of the poor to services administered at the state and local levels. In many cases the federal government is still far "closer" to the people in its capacity to protect the public interest from the relentless encroachment of a host of special interests that flourish in state capitals and city halls. This operational "closeness" must not be sacrificed on behalf of the Nixonian rhetoric of "returning government to the people."

—Federal help for states and local governments that today lack the staff resources and expertise that are needed to carry out a number of activities heretofore the principal responsibility of the federal government. This is especially true in regard to most state legislatures where the lack of professional staff, coupled with an appalling lack of experience, presents a distinctly foreboding picture.

—Agreement on a limited agenda of federal initiatives directed to the most urgent domestic priorities left unattended in the recent Nixon budget that cannot realistically be financed by state or local governments: national health insurance that initially focused on the medical needs of the poor (replacing Medicaid) and on catastrophic illness; housing allowances for persons who otherwise would qualify for public housing; welfare reform with income supplements for the working poor; and educational assistance for school districts with limited financial resources and great need.[13]

—A serious and sustained effort at tax reform with the dual objective of achieving a more equitable tax structure and additional sources of federal revenue to finance the more limited federal agenda. The joint proposal of Representative Wilbur Mills and Senator Mike Mansfield that fifty-four major tax

loopholes should expire over a three-year period unless continued by Congress makes good sense, shifting the burden of
proof to those who benefit from the special arrangements and
is exactly the kind of responsive legislative action that people can understand and appreciate. In the same vein, the public would also welcome a decision to lower social security
taxes for lower- and middle-income taxpayers, substituting
funds from general federal revenue.

None of these proposals suggests a less active or committed
federal government. Rather, they reflect a desire to use the
federal government's considerable leverage in ways more
likely to make sense to the electorate and drawing more fully
on the diversity of resources that exists outside the federal
bureaucracy.

The essential commitment of the Democratic Party, from
the New Deal until now, has been a willingness to *act* to
solve the nation's problems, particularly as these problems
are manifested in the daily lives of the American people. This
Democratic tradition must be dramatized at every opportunity.
In the post-Depression decades, this meant a direct, activist
role for the federal government at a time when well over a
third of the country's population was living below the poverty
line. Things are different today. The problems are different
and the mood of the country is different.

In short, the issue cannot remain liberal-versus-conservative
or federal activism–versus–returning government to the people. Democrats must force a new issue: *Which of the two
major parties is better able to achieve a new identity between
the activities of government and the needs of the people?*
Which of the two major parties is better able to communicate
this new identity in terms that the people can understand?

In attempting to define the politics of the 1970s in these
terms, Democrats should remember the following ground
rules:

1. Instead of instinctively thinking up new programs that
rely primarily on direct federal activism, Democrats should

be thinking up new ways to harness the power of the federal government to see that *problems* are solved, whether or not the federal government is directly involved. Financial sanctions, rewards and incentives, coupled with the creative use of the federal tax code, are instruments that should be explored as vital elements of this redefined federal activism.

2. Democrats should not, however, fall into the Nixon trap of attacking the federal government as seemingly the nation's principal threat to domestic tranquility. The people clearly do not hold this view. They understand that certain problems —such as health insurance and health care, welfare reform, educational help for poor school districts, and jobs for unemployable workers—will not be solved adequately without the federal government's taking the lead.

3. Democrats should always ask this question: Is it feasible to deliver on a governmental decision or action in ways that people can understand? Don't promise more and don't worry about admitting the limits of governmental action in a given situation. Candor counts above all else.

4. Avoid generalities; stick to specifics. The old shibboleths about the work ethic and federal paternalism are alive and well. The best path around these deadly political mines is to talk about specific, concrete cases, spelling out the human costs of President Nixon's approach and foresaking vague philosophical blasts about cuts in federal spending and retreats from social and economic justice. The issue is what happens in a specific community to specific problems that people encounter in their daily lives—not federal spending.

5. As a general rule, avoid singling out segments of the population as special problem groups requiring special attention. This does not signal a retreat from the Democratic Party's commitment to securing greater economic, political, and social justice in this country. But it does recognize that the most effective way to make real progress toward this goal is by mounting comprehensive governmental efforts to combat problems shared by a broad spectrum of citizens.

6. Democrats must not permit the White House or the Republican Party to preempt "Americanism"—the conventional

political morality that still flourishes in the hearts and minds
of most citizens. Democrats are *not* opposed to free enterprise,
or individual initiative, or personal civility, or the work ethic,
or safe streets, or loyalty to country. While the party was the
focal point of the anti-Vietnam War effort and the ideological
dormitory of the New Politics, it was all too easy for Republicans—American flags prominently affixed in their lapels—
seemingly to co-opt these values as their exclusive turf. The
Vietnam War has ended. Many of the New Politicians have
withdrawn to the West side of Manhattan. And Democrats
should make the most of it.

7. Democrats must not forget, or forsake, their traditional
advocacy of the economic concerns of the average working
family—consumer prices, jobs, interest rates, antitrust enforcement, consumer protection, and greater tax justice for lower-
and middle-income taxpayers. The sense that Democrats are
more committed to protecting the economic interests of the
average citizen is a good part of the glue that holds the New
Deal coalition together. The Republican Party, conversely, is
ill suited—by tradition, by instinct, by desire—to stand up for
these critical economic concerns, or so it seems to a substantial
plurality of the American electorate. Democrats must not
permit this distinction between the parties to become blurred.

8. Do not let Richard Nixon polarize the issues. For example, the President should not be allowed to juxtapose sim-
plistically the choice between increased taxes or "holding the
line on spending." Democrats should point to an affirmative
way that, in most cases, can appeal to the better instincts of
the American people. In the long run, the American public
will prove far more subtle and discriminating than traditional
Republicans believe it to be, *if* the Democrats are talking of
concrete solutions to specific problems that people can understand.

9. In addition to helping those persons who have yet to
make it economically and socially, Democrats must listen to
and act on the concerns of those Americans who *have* made

it but who quite properly expect a far greater level of responsiveness from their government and their elected officials. If the Democrats permit the Republicans to beat them at their own game of responding to popular needs, they deserve the fate predicted by Kevin Phillips and Richard Nixon.

6

THE
GOVERNING ISSUE

Apocalyptic predictions about the fate of the United States or the survival of democracy in America have lost much of their wallop over the course of the past decade, and properly so. For all its faults and shortcomings, the American political system has displayed considerable resilience and latent strength in these difficult years. Predictions of its imminent collapse have turned out to be wrong. In fact, the extraordinary outpouring of popular sentiment in response to the firing of Special Prosecutor Archibald Cox, and the related disposal of Attorney General Richardson and Deputy Attorney General Ruckelshaus, can only be seen as striking evidence of the underlying strength of representative democracy in the United States.

Then why describe the years 1974–76 as one last chance for the Democrats? The title of this book arises from the proposition that runs through its pages: Much of what ails political life in the United States today can be traced to a widening gulf between what citizens believe are their needs and what they see government doing in response to these needs. In part, these are the most basic sorts of needs: the price of groceries or the availability of home heating fuel. But other needs are less easy to define: How can life be made satisfying, more than just fair-to-middling? These feelings are not concentrated among Americans at the lower end of the socio-economic ladder, nor do they portend any lessening of popular affection for the United States as a country. As George Gallup reported in September 1973: "Although the vast ma-

jority [of Americans] indicates faith in the nation, it is doubtful that at any time in this century has politics commanded
so little respect."

If the linkages of trust and confidence that bind a people
to their government are wearing thin, the most effective way
to rebuild those linkages is through the political process. Political parties, especially in Congress and the states, must assume greater responsibility for translating popular concerns
into governmental action and for ensuring that governmental
bureaucracies deliver on goals that are set. But this effort will
require parties that are far stronger, far better organized, and
far more effective than the ones that exist today.

For the Democrats, at least, the next two years leading to
the bicentennial presidential election will be decisive in determining whether these expectations can be realized. Recent
history suggests that a sitting President, whether an Eisenhower, Kennedy, Johnson, or Nixon, can be a serious im-
pediment to building strong *party* institutions. Thus whatever serious efforts the Democrats intend to make toward reconstituting the party must be largely in place before the next
struggle for the presidential nomination begins in earnest. It
is in this sense that 1974 and 1975 offer the Democrats one
last chance to seize a unique political opportunity and turn
it to their long-term advantage.

Strong evidence suggests that the Democrats' cause is far
from hopeless. The base of a majority presidential coalition
survives demographically at the congressional level. Even as
they continue to espouse a generally conservative ideology that
extols personal initiative and derides governmental assistance,
the people also understand that most domestic problems cannot be resolved operationally without the involvement of the
federal government. But just as clearly, for the Democrats, the
application of federal power can no longer follow the traditional and often simplistic formulations of the New Deal
era or the sweeping moralisms of the New Politics. The previous chapter suggested a number of approaches to the use of
federal power that are less dependent upon direct federal
action and control and that do not rely upon the outmoded

ideological precepts of interest-group liberalism. More creative use of federal fiscal policy, for example, and heavier reliance on financial incentives and rewards—accompanied by strict standards of performance—to stimulate state and local action are elements of a new Democratic ideology.

But of greatest importance, the Democratic Party must bite the bullet of not seeming to promise something to everyone through the benevolence of the federal government. People are quite willing to accept the inherent limits of government action if the administration in power (1) focuses its energies on a limited agenda of priority matters that require federal involvement for solution, (2) uses federal power to equip other public and private institutions to attack more specialized problems, and (3) delivers on what it promises. There is a way to decide what merits priority attention at the federal level: through a political process composed of an active President, an invigorated Congress, strong governors, and strong state parties.

When the tumult, indictments, and convictions are over, the lasting damage to the Nixon Administration from Watergate will be its record of incompetence in permitting the sordid business to occur and its reliance on special favors and payoffs in raising funds for the 1972 Nixon presidential campaign. Gross incompetence and secret deals sit poorly with the voters. But the Democrats will not gain politically from these Republican troubles if their response is nothing more than loud and frequent proclamations about the immorality of the whole affair. Democrats will gain politically only to the extent that their own actions in the next two years help restore the popular trust and confidence that Watergate destroyed. It is of more than passing interest, in this regard, that the Gallup Poll of September 1973 reported Democratic Party allegiance holding steady at 43 per cent, Republicans dropping two points to 24 per cent, and independents increasing two points to 33 per cent.

The demonstration of Republican incompetence and special privilege arising from Watergate reinforces a more general view that President Nixon and his associates have been unable to manage the nation's economy—especially in controlling inflation—or handle the energy crisis, or combat crime and drug abuse, or clean up the environment, or devise a more equitable tax system. Again, the voters are left with a sense of incompetence and special privilege. One of President Nixon's more impressive, albeit unintended, political achievements has been to broaden the negative impact of the economic issue for the Republicans. Although there is ample evidence of GOP economic favoritism in corporate tax breaks and the operation of economic controls, the more comprehensive message is a pervasive dissatisfacton with Nixon economic programs that bridges those political gaps which traditionally separate the normal Democratic constituency from the Republican. If, as Scammon and Wattenberg suggest, contemporary American politics revolves around the economic and social issues, the Democrats at present appear to hold an advantage on the economic front and, at a minimum, to have neutralized the GOP's initial advantage on the social issue. But can the Democrats develop these political assets to the fullest, as the voters prepare to make their retrospective judgments in 1974 and 1976?

Overriding all else, data and analysis indicate the importance to the Democratic Party of focusing on what might be called the "Governing Issue." This issue involves two principal imperatives arising out of the last years of the Johnson Administration but brought to full flower under Richard Nixon: *first, to restore the popular belief that government—especially the federal government—can function competently and fairly; second, to convince people that government cares about what happens to average citizens.*

For Democrats, the Governing Issue has many dimensions. We have already considered the importance of evolving a new Democratic ideology to replace interest-group liberalism and of not creating expectations of governmental performance that are beyond realization. In the same spirit, Democrats should support the notion of the government's compensating individual citizens in cases of bureaucratic malfunctions, such as paying interest to taxpayers whose income tax refunds are unreasonably late. Opening the processes of government to greater public scrutiny, such as permitting television coverage of Congress, and full disclosure of all personal assets of elected officials are elements of the Governing Issue. Working toward a system of public financing of political campaigns is another. Representative Ella Grasso (D.—Conn.) is on the right track in proposing free postage for any citizen writing to a Member of Congress and installing her toll-free telephone line—the Ella phone—for constituents to call her congressional office. Governor Wendell Ford of Kentucky demonstrates his understanding of the Governing Issue when he spends several days at the state fair answering citizens' questions from a booth on the midway.

For Congress to recapture authority delegated to the executive branch and then to use that authority to control the executive is a dimension of the Governing Issue. A meaningful war powers bill, specific legislative authority to block unreasonable impoundments of appropriated funds, a tough budget control act to give Congress a voice in setting budget priorities, and stricter ground rules for the exercise of administrative power are ways for Congress to re-establish boundaries for presidential behavior. This is just another way of saying that everyone, even the President, has to play by the rules. Clear understanding of the Governing Issue would make Democrats simply say "No" to constituent groups demanding what is beyond the capability of government to provide.

A commitment to the Governing Issue does not involve the traditional reformer's cry to rise above party politics. To the contrary, it is only through a strengthened political process based on strong parties that meaningful development of the Governing Issue is possible. This is true for one reason: Political power exercised through party institutions is the way to make government operate effectively. A good politician, by definition, is one who understands the needs and desires of his or her constituents and who possesses the skill to translate those needs and desires into law or executive action. A strong political party gives the good politician the protection that often is required so he or she can also educate and lead a constituency. It is the absence of strong parties, in conjunction with the rise of the highly individualized exercise of political power in the Presidency and elsewhere, that makes possible excesses such as Watergate, along with the confusion and unresponsiveness in governmental action that erode the public's trust and confidence.

A conscious effort among Democrats to capitalize on the Governing Issue by moving beyond the precepts of interest-group liberalism is made easier by the changing composition of the party's national constituency. No longer can the party afford simply to focus its attention on the traditional elements of the New Deal coalition, even though these elements are necessary parts of a majority presidential coalition. If the party's functional constituency is defined as those persons who normally vote Democratic in congressional elections, it is clear that many of the standard notions about the party's composition need revision. As examined in the previous chapter, Democrats are infiltrating many demographic categories usually reserved for the GOP: higher-income families, the better-educated, middle-size cities and suburbs, and the middle-aged and older voters. To be sure, important elements of the FDR coalition remain, but it is no longer accurate to perceive the Democratic constituency solely in New Deal terms.

These trends make it less profitable politically for the party to design appeals that are tied directly to the specific demands of discrete social and economic groups. In terms of fully mobilizing the party's potential national constituency, Democrats must emphasize appeals that reflect problems of common popular experience and that can be solved by the even-handed application of law. This does *not* mean, however, that a specific problem of great urgency—such as the survival of public education in urban areas—should be denied the attention it obviously merits. But it does place two special obligations on the Democratic Party: first, to demonstrate to the electorate that such a problem ultimately affects the interests of all citizens, and second, to insist upon administrative procedures that deal fairly with all qualified persons and that eliminate special deals worked out informally with favored groups or individuals.

This more even-handed approach to designing and executing public policy will pay important political dividends in appealing to the growing army of independents who now constitute the nation's second largest "party." In the past decade, for example, persons calling themselves "Democrats" in the Gallup Poll have declined by six percentage points, "Republicans" have dropped one point, while "independents" have grown by seven points. The best way for Democrats to capture independent votes in any given election, as illustrated by the five races described in Chapter 3, is by stressing the key elements of the Governing Issue—competence, fairness, and concern on the part of government—while exploiting the usual Democratic advantage on the economic issue and neutralizing the social issue as a source of Republican strength. This strategy, if followed on the national level, would move millions of independents into the Democratic column.

A final and obvious proposition: If a strong party is a necessary factor in achieving these objectives, Democrats must devise internal procedures that strengthen and unify the party instead of weaken and divide it. This calls for a firm commitment to openness and fairness, but it also requires abandoning those artificial criteria, such as sex, age, or race, that led to the imposition of *de facto* quotas in the 1972 presidential nominating process. Nothing is more discriminatory, demeaning, or unfair than giving certain people an advantage over others on the basis of arbitrary demographic characteristics, assuming the operation of strictly enforced requirements on state parties and presidential candidates to seek out all groups and persons who have suffered discrimination in the past, including the 1972 campaign. Moreover, given the high levels of participation of women, youth, and minorities in the 1972 delegate-selection process, it is hard to believe that the party would slip back to the pre-1972 levels if quotas were ruled out in 1976.

The evolution of *de facto* quotas in the 1969–72 period should be seen as an extreme consequence of the ideology of interest-group liberalism applied to internal Democratic Party issues. By the same token, the recommendations of the Commission on Delegate Selection established by the 1972 National Convention to abandon quotas, adopted in October 1973, represent the party's first explicit step toward a more even-handed management of its own business and the most definitive rejection of a strategy, however well-intentioned, that ended up offering special consideration for certain groups. This decision to move away from the quota experiment was coupled with strict requirements on the state parties for procedural fairness and affirmative steps to involve groups that had been discriminated against in earlier times. This change in delegate-selection rules is an example of the precepts of the Governing Issue being applied *within* the Democratic Party.

The delegate-selection procedures for 1976 should also ensure at the next national convention an adequate presence of Democrats who have won elective public office. Unlike persons who might be awarded delegate seats on the basis of quotas, elected Democratic officials have already presented themselves to the electorate and can claim legitimacy as national convention participants on that basis. Elected officials also tend to be year-round Democrats who assume much of the responsibility for the day-to-day business of maintaining the party and running the country. Their active participation in nominating the party's candidates and writing the platform is obviously desirable.

But the choice is not between the pre-1972 delegate-selection procedures that contained serious elements of unfairness and party rules blind to the needs of organization and expertise. It is quite feasible to have an open party and fair nominating rules without losing a third of the normal Democratic constituency in the process. Rules can be written that give ample opportunity for the expression of grassroots sentiment without driving out the year-round Democrats, the most reliable spokesmen for "casual Democrats" who make the difference between victory and defeat on Election Day. Democrats, in short, can no longer initiate internal reforms without taking into account the impact of their actions on party structure and organization. *Rules for 1976 must be written from the dual perspective of selecting the nominee in a fair and*

*open manner and of strengthening the party to enable the
nominee not only to win the Presidency but also to govern
effectively.* Once this dual perspective is accepted, a number
of workable and fair procedures are possible. (The author's
proposals for delegate-selection rules, as well as for reconstituting the national and state Democratic parties, are contained
in the Appendix, "A Democrat's Notebook," which follows
this chapter.)

The Democratic Party must become a significant factor in
the nomination and election of candidates and in the forma-
tion and execution of public policy. This requires state
Democratic parties, in particular, to acquire the capability of
recruiting candidates for public office and then helping them
win election. It means state parties that provide a real alternative in services and expertise to the independent political
consultants who deal directly with individual candidates. With
rare exceptions, however, state party organizations have almost vanished and need help from the national party if they
are to revive. The successful Democratic national telethon in
September 1973 operated on a formula allocating one-half
the money to state parties, a sensible precedent for the future
in reconstituting moribund state organizations. In regard to
public financing of campaigns, it is essential that parties play
a role in dispensing whatever funds eventually are made
available. To circumvent parties in the public funding process
would be to offer a positive incentive for the irresponsible
exercise of political power by elected officials.

There is an obvious need for more forceful and imaginative
party leadership in Congress: to strengthen the institutions
of party control, such as the caucus, to settle on a limited
agenda of priority legislation, to round up the votes that are
needed to pass it, and to speak out more frequently in behalf
of the Democratic congressional party. We hear a lot of talk
these days about the importance of "citizens' lobbies." Congress potentially is the most effective citizens' lobby in Washington. If the Democratic Party leadership would seize the
Governing Issue as its principal political blueprint, the link
between an elected representative and his or her constituents,

as magnified by a forceful party agenda of people-oriented legislation, should prove far more durable and effective than relationships growing out of voluntary membership organizations, such as Common Cause—useful as they are in alerting people to their duties as citizens. Strengthened political parties in the states are vital to the process; congressional leaders must include governors and other state officials as full-fledged participants in drawing up and enacting a Democratic Party program. The end result, as noted in Chapter 1, is a balance: vigorous presidential leadership confronted by congressional spokesmen who bring significant expertise and perspective to the public dialogue.

These steps toward enlarging the party's role nationally and in the states need not be at the expense of the local base that has given the American political system both its flexibility and its long-term stability. It makes no sense whatever to talk in terms of a highly centralized and disciplined party system. That is completely alien to American political experience. But, again, the choice is not between absolute control by national party institutions and utter chaos. There are ways to preserve the strong ties between elected officials and their local constituents and still achieve a more focused sense of direction by the larger party. Some are spelled out in the Appendix.

The prime factor in achieving a balance between internal order and responsiveness to local concerns is a stronger sense of the Democratic Party's *purpose* in America today: to win elections, of course—political parties are not in business to lose. But the path to victory for the Democrats in the mid-1970s is a more profound understanding of the Governing Issue—its substance, its potential appeal to the electorate, and its significance in building a more esteemed political system in America. This book has sought to lay the groundwork for an understanding of the Governing Issue, to define it, and to translate it into specific decisions and directions that should be taken by the Democratic Party prior to 1976 in order to restore governmental competence, fairness, and concern for the individual in the years following. Democrats could do

worse than build their next presidential campaign on the
theme, "Let's make democracy work once again—for all the
people."

As the final words of this book were written in late fall
1973, President Nixon was generally thought to be in desperate
trouble, and his continuation in office for the balance of his
second term was in doubt. Whether or not the President will
survive his many crises cannot be known. But there has
already arisen among some Democrats a disturbing assumption: Nixon's trouble in 1973 is certain to translate into
Democratic success in 1976. Among Democrats who ought to
know better, there exists the sense of inevitable victory that
infected the party in the aftermath of the unexpected Democratic showing in 1970. To recall the words of George Mc-
Govern in January 1973: "I firmly believed throughout 1971
that the major hurdle to winning the Presidency was winning
the Democratic nomination. I believed that any reasonable
Democrat could defeat President Nixon."

The fact is that, if the Democrats seriously hope to win the
Presidency in 1976, they must demonstrate a capacity to
govern. A strengthened Democratic Party, committed to the
implementation of the Governing Issue, is the only strategy for
defeating a possible Ford-Richardson or Richardson-Ford
ticket (or some other attractive combination) and winning the
White House. This means that Democrats must set about
getting their own house in order now, so that the battle for
the nomination can go forward without the internecine strife
of 1968 and 1972. It means evolving a governing strategy that
attracts the support of a majority of the electorate. This is
the bottom line of the Governing Issue.

Entirely too much time and attention are still being devoted
to speculation about the identity of the next Democratic presidential nominee. Entirely too little concern is being expressed
over the character of the party that person will represent. The
times demand a nominee who can himself wholeheartedly
subscribe to and embody the substance of the Governing
Issue—a person who is prepared to conduct his Presidency on
the basis of competence, fairness, and concern for the in-

dividual citizen. This Democrat is the only kind who can win in 1976. This President is the kind we must have to inaugurate America's third century as a free nation.

In effect, we are talking about a new public philosophy for America—a task that traditionally has fallen to the Democratic Party and its leaders. Will this tradition be honored in the election years of 1974 and 1976? That is the question Democrats must answer before America celebrates its 200th birthday.

APPENDIX:
A DEMOCRAT'S
NOTEBOOK

Parties are potentially the most effective link between citizens and their government. Winning politics in the
mid–70s therefore cannot be limited to the decisions and
actions that produce victory on Election Day. A politician who
wants to stay a winner must engage the public's trust not only
in the campaign but equally in the intervening months and
years between campaigns—a much more difficult job. The
lesson of the past several administrations can be simply re-
stated: Political leaders at all levels—in the cities and towns,
the states, and in Congress as well as the White House—must
take a more direct hand in securing competence, fairness, and
individual concern in the workings of government.

It is obvious that, to the degree the national Democratic
Party occupies itself with divisive and time-consuming internal
problems, it will be less able to focus on external concerns of
citizens' problems and public policy. But because there has
been a lengthy and necessary preoccupation in the Democratic
Party with internal problems, these also need to be reviewed
and commented on. The sections that follow represent this
Democrat's observation of reform efforts already completed or
in process as this book was written. They are cast in the light
of the data and analysis assembled for the book, but they
also reflect personal convictions—not susceptible of precise
verification—about the need to strengthen the national Democratic Party in ways that will make it a more effective force in
governing the nation, without overlooking the need to win

elections. They assume no radical transformation of the American political party system itself.

THE COMMISSION ON DELEGATE SELECTION

A resounding Democratic victory in 1974 would be one sign of the party's recovery from the trauma of 1972. Another indication would be a new perspective on internal party reform in the work of the Commission on Delegate Selection created by the 1972 National Convention. Progress in bringing together the reformers and regulars on the question of delegate selection would be an explicit indication of a political maturity that was conspicuously absent in 1968 and 1972.

In 1968 the reformers adopted the strategy that a Democratic loss to Richard Nixon would teach the regulars a lesson. In 1972 many of the regulars adopted the same posture toward the reformers. By now, both factions should have learned the real lesson: Neither side can hope to win without the other. The actions of the Commission on Delegate Selection can be seen as the initial barometer of whether this lesson has indeed been learned.

The National Convention's resolution establishing the 116-member Commission on Delegate Selection, chaired by Barbara Mikulski, a member of the Baltimore City Council, set forth three major duties: (1) reviewing the 1972 delegate-selection guidelines and making "appropriate revision," (2) adopting new guidelines "to fully implement the Call to the 1976 Democratic National Convention," and (3) monitoring the affirmative efforts of the national and state Democratic parties "to achieve full participation of minorities, youth and women" in the delegate-selection process and all party affairs.

The first solid clue to suggest that a new political maturity might be emerging over the question of delegate selection came in a statement by Senator George McGovern before the first meeting of the Charter Commission of the Democratic Party in April 1973. In a remarkable change from his earlier views on party reform, McGovern urged the elimination of all quotas, *de facto* or otherwise, and he advocated greater control by presidential candidates or other party leaders in drawing up slates of delegates, the precise issue over which Mayor Daley and his Chicago delegates were sent packing. McGovern said, in part, that

> . . . we need not pretend that the reforms were written in stone. Every sound law must be informed and improved by experience. Human rules will fail sometimes, for human beings are frail always. And the reform rules were not without some defects or errors of interpretation even as they are properly judged a general success.
>
> Criticism of the reforms appears to fall within two broad areas—first, the problems of what proved in some cases to be a quota system for the selection of delegates—and second, the fear, shared by some Democrats, that the system operated to deprive the Convention of the work and wisdom of the party's most senior leaders. . . .
>
> I think two specific changes in the reform rules are in order. First, the phrase "reasonable relationship to their presence in the population of the state" should be removed from the guidelines. That will eliminate the misunderstanding that led to the imposition of quotas while leaving intact the language requiring affirmative action to insure full and fair representation. . . .
>
> Second, we should also seek a delegate selection system that truly reflects the preference of Democratic voters. "Widespread participation in the slate-making process" should not be construed to require surrender of the slate-making power by presidential candidates.
>
> The party should amend its guidelines to secure the right of presidential candidates to protect the integrity of the method that chooses delegates in their name. The same right should be granted to party organizations or any other group that decides to run a slate independently. . . .
>
> [A]ll of us want to win again—not by looking wistfully to the past—but by welcoming the future.
>
> Democrats have made mistakes, and there is surely blame enough for everyone, including me. During the last six years, we have wasted so much of ourselves in factional dispute and disarray. Now it is our common mission to prepare, not just for the next election, but the next generation.

This shift in position was important because it suggested that a person's commitment to the goal of an open party and to fairness in selecting convention delegates no longer had to be judged by the specific criteria laid down by the most militant reformers. McGovern was criticized bitterly by some of the militants, but his statement was a signal to the rest of the party that a normal process of compromise and accommodation was possible in writing the rules for 1976.

Following a summer of public hearings to solicit ideas from all elements of the party, the Delegate Selection Commission met in Washington in September 1973 for its first meeting of all the members. Differences quickly surfaced between the activist reformers and the regulars on such questions as mandatory quotas, slate-making, *ex officio* delegates, and proportional representation. The regulars challenged the authority of the commission to promulgate final delegate-selection rules and declared that only the Democratic National Committee itself could make those decisions. The reformers asserted their obligation to report only to the 1976 National Convention and threatened to take the DNC to federal court if any of the commission's decisions were changed. A distinct aroma of moral certitude could be noted in the debate, and the hope of achieving an acceptable compromise between the warring factions seemed to vanish.

A drafting committee met subsequently in Washington for two weekend sessions. By late October the full commission reconvened to consider the drafting committee's recommendations. To almost everyone's astonishment, the commission adopted them unanimously. This extraordinary and unexpected turnabout demands closer examination. What did the drafting committee decide? How was it possible to bridge the differences that had separated the regulars from the reformers barely more than one month earlier?

In essence, the capacity to compromise (a way of recognizing that your opponent might be right) returned to the Democratic Party. The most difficult issues turned out to be the regulars' demand for the explicit rejection of mandatory quotas in the selection of convention delegates versus the demand by black participants that their newly won prominence in national party affairs not be sacrificed by abandoning the

1972 rules. Both demands turned out to be negotiable—a marked transformation from the non-negotiating era of the late 1960s and early 1970s.

The blacks, principally represented on the drafting committee by Mayor Richard Hatcher of Gary, Indiana, eventually acquiesced in the rejection of mandatory quotas as a way of bringing minorities into the delegate-selection process. The regulars, whose most effective spokesman turned out to be Governor John Gilligan of Ohio, agreed to a tough, enforceable program of affirmative action that is likely to have considerable impact on the structure and procedures of state Democratic parties. A seventeen-member Compliance Review Commission was created to judge whether state parties have adopted meaningful affirmative-action and delegate-selection programs and have implemented them in delegate selection. But, once a state party has been judged to be in compliance on those two grounds, national convention delegations will no longer be subject to challenge solely on the basis of the delegation's composition.

Other factors came into play. Members of the drafting committee not only *listened* to what their opponents were saying but also refrained from rejecting these views out of hand. Example: The regulars objected to the practice of McGovern supporters in some states of attending more than one precinct caucus—a movable majority, so to speak. The rules now explicitly forbid anyone from attending more than one precinct caucus. The reformers could not help but take account of the 1972 presidential election results and Senator McGovern's proposals for amending the rules for 1976. The regulars, however, were forced to recognize the political skills of the reformers in winning the nomination in 1972, as well as their continuing commitment to the party. The feeling on either side that the party would be "better off" without the opposing side had been diminished considerably by the Nixon landslide.

Both regulars and reformers could count their victories in the drafting committee's recommendations. The rules were unyielding in their commitment to an open party and the necessity of fair procedures at each step in the delegate-selection process. But the absolute ban against proxy voting was relaxed. Slate-making by presidential candidates or other party groups was approved (a major victory for the regulars, as well as one of Senator McGovern's suggestions). The regulars' proposal for the appointment of *ex officio* voting delegates—governors and U.S. senators and representatives—was rejected, although the Democratic National Committee was urged to extend "privileges" to such dignitaries. The percentage of delegates chosen by state committees was increased from ten to twenty-five, thereby making it possible to appoint to the delegation groups that were shortchanged in the election process. But stringent requirements were laid down for selecting the state committee "through open processes in conformity with the basic procedural guarantees utilized for delegate selection." A procedure was approved for the fair reflection of presidential preferences in the allocation of delegate strength, another way of saying that the winner-take-all primary was banned. It was agreed that delegates would be elected from districts no larger than a congressional district and that advisory presidential-preference primaries would not affect the selection of delegates. An apportionment formula for delegates within states was adopted that permitted state parties to choose between the approach favored by the reformers and the one favored by the regulars. State parties were instructed to take all feasible steps to restrict participation in the delegate-selection process to Democratic voters only, an effort to eliminate the open or crossover primaries in which Republicans and independents help select the Democratic Party's nominee.

In short, the Delegate Selection Commission attempted to correct the worst abuses of 1972 without sacrificing the spirit or commitment that motivated the 1972 reforms. It would be premature, however, to assume that this achievement necessarily signals a new era of peace and tranquility among Democrats. The regulars and reformers voted for the drafting committee's text for different reasons (some of the regulars hope to win additional changes from the Democratic National

Committee, and the reformers believed a unanimous report by the commission would be their best defense against such subsequent changes). Spirited contests for the control of state Democratic committees can be expected, as can disagreements over the content and implementation of affirmative-action plans in specific states. The regulars generally regard the duties of the newly established Compliance Review Commission as a way of keeping credentials challenges from the doorstep of the 1976 National Convention (the CRC is directed to settle all disputes over affirmative-action and delegate-selection plans prior to initiation of the state's delegate-selection process). But the reformers tend to view the Compliance Review Commission as a device to insure the adequate representation of blacks and other minorities on the delegations. The resolution of these conflicting perspectives, likely to occur in mid- to late 1975, will generate more heat than light in some states.

There is, in other words, considerable opportunity for internecine strife to resume. Whether the spirit of the Delegate Selection Commission's efforts can be sustained in 1974 and 1975 will be a critical test of the party's seriousness about winning the Presidency in 1976.

THE CHARTER COMMISSION

That a Charter Commission exists at all is testimony to the shift in attitudes toward internal reform that took place between February 1971, when the delegate-selection guidelines were adopted unanimously, and the convening of the Democratic National Convention in July 1972.

In a final effort to take advantage of the reform momentum that had been generated after 1968, the McGovern-Fraser Commission and the O'Hara Commission, having completed their original assignments, jointly prepared a national charter of the Democratic Party for submission to the National Convention. The charter grew out of the deeply held conviction that existing party institutions were no longer capable of serving the true needs of the American people or the nation itself.

Modernization and renovation were urgently needed. In the words of the report accompanying the proposed charter: "The members . . . are not prepared to dismiss the two-party system as an anachronism. We believe that system has served this nation well, and can continue to do so. It will require, as it has required in every generation since Jefferson founded it and Jackson perfected it, updating and modernization."

The charter was designed to provide, for the first time in American political history, a national framework of organization for a major party and a far more explicit relationship between individual Democrats and the operations of party institutions. The leading advocates of the proposal, Representatives Donald Fraser and James O'Hara, frankly admitted that it represented an attempt to build a more responsible and centralized party structure usually associated with parliamentary systems of government. They urged such innovations as formal membership in the Democratic Party, a new national hierarchy of party institutions beginning on the congressional district level and culminating in the national convention, a 3,000-delegate National Policy Conference in the even-numbered years between presidential elections, and a National Executive Committee consisting of the national party chairman, the Senate and House Democratic leaders, regional Democratic chairmen, and representatives of state and local governments.

Without going into detail, suffice it to say that such a departure from the traditional concept of loosely structured, highly decentralized parties was more than a lot of Democrats were ready to buy, particularly in the period where the controversies arising from the delegate-selection reforms were being thrashed out. The AFL-CIO, in particular, worked diligently against its adoption in 1972. The House Democratic caucus also passed a resolution opposing the charter document.

Rather than attempt the complicated, if not impossible, job of hammering out an acceptable compromise in the midst of an already overworked convention, the charter advocates agreed to the creation of a commission "to consider and recommend a permanent charter for the Democratic Party of the United States" and to recommend to the Democratic National Committee the size, composition, and manner of electing delegates to a party conference in 1974 that would act on the charter recommendation and other business. In addition, the National Convention adopted a comprehensive restructuring of the Democratic National Committee along the lines proposed by the charter advocates. Postponing the more controversial aspects of the proposal until 1974 was an obvious way to avoid another bruising struggle that could only have driven the wedge deeper between Senator McGovern and the party's established leadership.

Charter Commission Chairman Terry Sanford, former governor of North Carolina and now president of Duke University, and his 160-member commission face an important and delicate assignment. Objections to the initial charter proposal fell into two broad categories: (1) opposition to the concept of enrolled party membership because, in the view of many Democrats, it would restrict and weaken rather than expand and strengthen the party's popular base; and (2) opposition to what many Democratic leaders saw as excessive grassroots control of the national party hierarchy and an insufficient role for elected public and party officials.

If these were the only problems to be resolved, the Charter Commission could look forward to a relatively uneventful tenure. Such is not likely to be the case. A more fundamental issue has been raised: the degree of uniformity and control that a national party, however organized, can—and should—impose upon state and local Democratic parties and leaders. Even firm advocates of national action in meeting many domestic problems have their doubts about the thrust of the initial charter. As Senator McGovern said in his comments at the Charter Commission's organizational meeting in April 1973: "I have found also that in our party, as in our country, there is strength in diversity. Therefore, I oppose an enforced conformity of rules except where the principles or progress of the whole party are at stake."

On the other hand, the data in the earlier chapters of this book clearly suggest that this is no time for business as usual by either of the two major parties. Disenchantment with both parties and their leaders is growing, as is a general malaise and dissatisfaction with the tenor of our national life. "On every side," says the report on the national charter, "we are told that party loyalties and party affiliations are dying, to be replaced by the politics of personality and charisma."

To address this problem creatively is the Charter Commission's great challenge and opportunity. It will require, above all else, a disposition to take the Democratic Party seriously, not only as an organization to win elections but as an instrument in governing the nation. This the McGovern-Fraser and O'Hara commissions clearly did in their proposed charter. While there was much disagreement with specific provisions of their plan, there can be little doubt of their goal of restoring the Democratic Party to a position where it could deal more responsibly with America's most urgent problems.

This goal can be achieved more effectively if two distinct tasks are explicitly recognized: (1) the restoration of the national and state Democratic parties as competent electoral organizations, capable in their own right of recruiting attractive candidates and helping them win public office, and (2) the gradual evolution of the national Democratic Party into a more responsible instrument in the formulation and implementation of public policy, an objective that necessarily involves the party structures in Congress, the Democratic governors, and the state legislatures. The first job should receive priority attention in the work of the Charter Commission, if only for the reason that demonstrated political muscle is an effective way of bringing a higher degree of responsibility to the conduct of Democratic public officials.

Two general problems are at the root of the party's deficiencies as an effective campaign organization, nationally and in the states: (1) the absence of a productive and reliable system of political fund-raising and (2) the inability to command the most sophisticated campaign techniques and tools except as they are made available by independent campaign consultants under contract to individual candidates with the money to purchase them, along with the failure to conduct systematic education and training of campaign workers that would vastly increase their ability to win elections. It is obvious that solving the first problem, political fund-raising, would be a major step toward solving the second.

The initial charter called for the creation of a National Membership and Finance Council composed of one member from each state and twenty members-at-large. The council was to work with the Democratic National Committee in establishing state financial quotas and in organizing national and state fund-raising campaigns. Most state Democratic parties use only the most primitive techniques in raising money, and even those in a sporadic and highly unpredictable fashion. None of the state parties feels the slightest obligation to assist the Democratic National Committee in its difficult financial circumstances. As a result, the only serious fund-raising is carried on by individual candidates who somehow, somewhere get the money they need to run for office. The Democratic Party—nationally and in the states—has no choice but to pick up what is left, which usually isn't much.

But it doesn't have to be this way. One of the unqualified successes of the McGovern campaign was its reliance on small contributions and its imaginative use of direct-mail and newspaper advertising to reach potential givers. Response to McGovern's appeal for small contributions tripled the previous record for grassroots giving set by the Goldwater campaign of 1964. In September 1973, the Democratic National Committee conducted a highly successful fund-raising telethon on NBC that raised $5.5 million from 575,000 contributors. The net proceeds were divided evenly between the DNC and the states where the money was raised.

Another dimension of the finance problem is, of course, the question of public financing of campaigns. There is already on the books a federal law authorizing the public financing of the 1976 presidential campaign if a sufficient number of federal taxpayers designate one dollar of their personal income taxes to a presidential campaign fund and if Congress votes to release the money. The Nixon Administration, however, succeeded in burying the forms for the dollar check-off in the

1972 tax returns and, as a consequence, only about 4 per cent of the taxpayers made the required designation. Congress has now demanded that the Internal Revenue Service provide an easy and obvious procedure for using the dollar check-off on 1973 tax returns before any final judgments are made. In the wake of Watergate, Congress is also considering a range of new proposals for broader public financing of political campaigns, but prospects for the passage of any of them are far from certain.

The process will be evolutionary at best. Funds are likely to be available in actual campaign periods only and not on a year-round basis to support other party activities. Therefore, the Charter Commission should give special attention to devising a financial structure that would require cooperative fund-raising by the national and state parties—such as occurred on the national telethon—with professional staff using proven fund-raising techniques. Once the party's financial picture brightens, as it can through continuing and systematic effort, it becomes relatively easy to hire the staff and acquire the facilities for the Democratic Party to wage thoroughly professional political campaigns and to offer the year-round education, training, and service components.

As to the second task—the growth of the national Democratic Party into a more responsible instrument in the formulation and implementation of public policy—one must question the feasibility of any proposal, however attractive in theory, that fails to take account of the natural diversity of constituents and interests that inevitably exists within a majority presidential coalition. Not only does such a proposal run counter to the entire history of American parties, but it goes in the opposite direction of striving for greater decentralization and flexibility in the relationship of the federal government to the states and localities.

A rigid party structure, starting at the congressional district level and funneling upward to a national convention, a national policy conference, and a national executive committee, would necessarily involve the top-level party leaders in a never-ending process of deciding national policy issues with no assurance that these decisions would be accepted by the Democratic leadership in Congress, by the Democratic governors and mayors, and by the state parties. If the national party possessed the authority and power to control the nominating process for Congress and state and local offices, then its decisions could be enforced more readily. But no one, to my knowledge, has argued for this degree of centralization, nor could anyone expect to achieve it in the foreseeable future. In short, it makes little sense to talk seriously about creating a Democratic Party structure that requires a high degree of centralized power to be functional. And, lacking this power, such a structure is apt to exacerbate differences rather than encourage the process of accommodating divergent interests.

Two recent developments offer hope that a greater degree of party responsibility is possible without having to attempt the kind of sweeping structural reforms contained in the original charter. Congress is gradually evolving a more effective system of party leadership and party responsibility. The willingness to adopt party positions on controversial issues is growing, even within the diversity that still characterizes the congressional parties in the Senate and House. And, for the first time in Democratic Party history, the National Committee itself is a fairly representative body, not only in the categories of members—national committeemen and women, state party chairmen and vice chairmen, members of Congress, governors, mayors, state legislators, and private groups, such as organized labor—but in the proportional voting strength that now exists among the states. (Prior to the 1972 reform of the National Committee structure, every state and territory had two votes, regardless of size.)

The Democratic National Committee now has the potential of speaking for the national Democratic Party, at least on general issues and priorities. This is not a role that the current Democratic National Chairman, Robert S. Strauss, believes should occupy the National Committee to any significant extent. But the current situation should not blind the Charter Commission to the important new instrument in party affairs that the National Committee now represents. There is no reason why the DNC could not evolve, over time, into a significant voice in the affairs of the nation.

The national party conference, now scheduled for early December 1974 to consider and adopt the proposed charter, is also a forum for considering broader questions of public policy. Initially, DNC Chairman Strauss and Democratic congressional leaders intended to limit the conference agenda to consideration of the charter question. This view has now been modified to include selected policy questions approved by the Democratic National Committee. The conference will be composed of grassroots Democrats elected as delegates in 1974 and all Democratic governors and U.S. senators and representatives. It is an ideal forum to give meaning and substance to the Governing Issue as the party begins serious preparation for winning the Presidency in 1976.

STRENGTHENING THE CONGRESSIONAL PARTY

In one of the recurring ironies of American politics, the U.S. Congress—controlled, as usual, by the Democrats—initiated the most sweeping changes since the early 1900s in its structure and procedure in the wake of a presidential campaign in which the loser's poor showing was due, at least in the minds of many persons, to an excess of political reform. If, as some commentators suggested, the political mood of the country was one of retrenchment and protecting the old order, these feelings somehow seemed to have escaped the notice of congressional Democrats and Republicans upon their return to Washington in January 1973.

The changes took place, in part, because a growing number of congressional reform advocates—inside and outside of Congress—had worked for years and were better organized to act during 1973 than ever before. These changes can also be traced, in part, to the fact that Congress is in the midst of a sweeping demographic revolution: Half of the House of Representatives has come to Capitol Hill since 1967, and forty-five out of one hundred senators were not holding office six years ago. Only a third of the Democrats in Congress have more than ten years of seniority. So, possessing little themselves, these younger members of Congress are notoriously uneasy over such traditions as seniority and actively impatient with legislative procedures that excessively hamper the formulation of something resembling a coherent legislative program.

To be sure, the congressional reform process was helped along by President Nixon's concerted effort either to usurp what Congress believed were its constitutional prerogatives or simply to ignore Congress in his management, or dismemberment, of the executive branch. For the first time in years, Congress gave some evidence of a new determination to fight back.

Congress—especially the House of Representatives—made a number of positive changes in 1973. These changes fell into two broad categories: (1) changes that contributed to the openness and responsiveness of the institution and (2) changes that strengthened the elected party leadership at the expense of the standing committee chairmen. Both categories of change should be seen by the Democrats as positive steps in developing the Governing Issue—that is, in helping the party respond more directly to the public's growing cynicism toward government that exists concurrently with a desire for greater governmental competence and responsiveness, for a greater concern for individual problems, and its much tougher attitude toward the government's failure to deliver on its promises.

With the active encouragement and support of Speaker Carl Albert, Democrats in the House took the following steps in a frantic burst of activity during the early weeks of 1973:

—Opened to the public all meetings of House committees and subcommittees where bills are voted on, and all committee and subcommittee hearings, unless a majority of the committee votes by roll call to close them. This means that the critical "mark-up" stage of drafting legislation—when the committee members vote on specific provisions of a bill—can be open to public scrutiny unless a majority of the committee takes the explicit step of closing the session. This is a change of far-reaching importance since it stops members from saying one thing publicly and doing something else in the closed committee meetings.

—Required a vote of approval by the Democratic caucus on all committee chairmen, thereby abandoning the tradition where seniority was the sole criterion in filling committee chairmanships. This guarantees to the party leadership and the caucus a chance to depose committee chairmen who consistently obstruct the legislative program or ignore the views of Democrats on the committees or in the caucus.

—Established a Democratic Policy Committee, composed of principal party leaders and other House members, to recommend legislative priorities and party policy to the Democratic caucus and the committees. This establishes a direct link between Democratic members and the party leadership; it is a considerable change from the days when Speaker Sam Rayburn met in the late afternoon with his friends in what reporters termed the "board of education" to decide what the House should be doing.

—Guaranteed one major committee and subcommittee assignment for every Democrat in the House, regardless of seniority.

—Suspended the use of a "closed rule," a parliamentary device for preventing amendments on the House floor to certain types of legislation, such as tax bills, if a majority of the Democratic caucus votes to permit specific floor amendments. This means that amendments that otherwise could be bottled up in committee can be offered on the floor for a vote by the full House, a change that further increases the power of party leaders and the Democratic caucus over committee chairmen.

In the Senate the changes were less sweeping, in part because the institution is less dependent on rigid parliamentary rules and procedure. Senate committee chairmen were made subject to caucus approval every two years and all committees were authorized to hold open sessions if a majority of the committee members requested. But the Senate mounted a more aggressive response to what was viewed as the unconstitutional usurpation of its legislative powers by President Nixon and the executive branch.

Senator Sam Ervin of North Carolina, when he was not chairing sessions of the Watergate select committee, took the lead in restricting the scope of executive privilege as interpreted by the Nixon Administration and in limiting the President's power to impound funds appropriated by the Congress for specific federal activities. The Senate Democratic Policy Committee accepted the difficult assignment of drawing up a "counterbudget" to Nixon's $268.7 billion federal budget for fiscal year 1974—holding federal spending to the $12.7 billion deficit proposed by the President but shifting funds from military and foreign aid to domestic areas. Majority Leader Mike Mansfield began meeting regularly with Speaker Carl Albert to coordinate the legislative agendas of the respective houses. And swirling around these developments were other events that dominated the daily headlines: the rising clamor over the Watergate investigation, the secret bombing of Cambodia, the congressionally imposed halt to military actions in Southeast Asia, the energy crisis, and the Administration's continuing struggle with the economy. A session that had opened with a Republican President fully in charge and the Democratic Congress dispirited and leaderless had swung around in less than four months' time: the President in the worst personal crisis of his Administration—his policies at home and abroad under severe attack—facing a Democratic Congress that had taken a number of long-overdue steps to improve its capacity to act and had moved to the offensive in certain areas.

All of this, however, must be kept in perspective. The ultimate effect of Watergate on the Nixon Presidency at this writing is unknown. And the changes in congressional procedures are significant primarily because they are hopeful signs of life in a period when one might have expected from Congress further retreat and retrenchment. But it is also likely that these changes will have less impact on the House and Senate than their most ardent supporters have suggested. Speaker Al-

bert and, to a lesser degree, Senator Mansfield have taken
a more active role in leading the congressional party, but
Democrats in neither house have succeeded in developing a
true sense of collective responsibility for their actions. There
remains in most situations an overriding commitment to indi-
vidualism, regardless of the effect individual actions have on
the party's ability to achieve its legislative objectives. In this
sense, then, the reforms of the 93d Congress are only a beginning, albeit a good beginning, toward a greater degree of
party responsibility.

If the problems of the Nixon Presidency deepen in 1974
and 1975, the Democrats could well be faced with a truly his-
toric challenge: that of assuming major responsibility for running the country in the face of an enfeebled and powerless
President. If these circumstances should develop, the Democrats will be forced into several of the postures advocated in
this book: a willingness to move away from the familiar solutions of the New Deal and Great Society, a redefinition of the
Democratic Party's purpose in today's society along the lines
suggested by the Governing Issue, and a more certain grasp of
the notion that governmental performance is the key to electoral success for the balance of the 1970s. The most one can
say at this juncture is that the reforms and initiatives of early
1973 reveal a recognition among congressional Democrats that
the old ways are no longer sufficient and that a capacity to
change does exist.

The Democratic National Committee

The day-to-day politics of the Democratic National Committee is a rather esoteric subject, understood by few people
and for good reason: Most of the perpetual infighting involves only those persons and interests with a stake in what
the National Committee itself does and related only infer-
entially and indirectly to broader political concerns. But if
one can step out of the minutiae, the job of Democratic National Chairman Robert S. Strauss is not hard to define: to
persuade everyone to keep their knives under the table, at
least in public meetings, and to devise ways to use the 303

National Committee members and their respective constituencies in accomplishing five major tasks:

(1) to complete the remaining reform agenda without undue public controversy and commotion, a job that can be made much easier if Democrats retain some perspective on the larger questions that face the party
(2) to make a creditable showing in the 1974 congressional and gubernatorial elections as hard evidence of the party's recovery from the presidential debacle of 1972
(3) to establish a more solid financial base of support for year-round education and service activities that are essential in rebuilding party organizations nationally and in the states
(4) to provide an opportunity for the national party to take official recognition of the new ideological directions that, it is hoped, will begin to replace the concepts of interest-group liberalism
(5) to devise more effective ways—in Congress, in the states and from the Democratic National Committee—to get the party's message through to the American electorate

Strauss was elected chairman of the National Committee in December 1972 because he had done a good job as national treasurer during Lawrence F. O'Brien's tenure as national chairman (1970–72), because he wanted the job, and because he worked harder than anyone else to get it.

With the active support of most Democratic governors and the political apparatus of the AFL-CIO, Strauss won a hard-fought victory, emphasizing throughout that he would not turn back the clock on reform, that he was not an "ideologue," and that he intended to work with all wings, factions, segments, and caucuses within the Democratic Party. Recent history suggests the extreme difficulty of realizing this goal: The basic interests of George McGovern, George Wallace, and George Meany, for example, appear too divergent to be contained under one political umbrella, even if it is held by a man as persuasive and nonideological as Robert Strauss.

It is, of course, too early for any final judgments about

whether the three Georges can learn to live together, even though it is not premature to suggest that the Democrats will find it difficult to win in 1976 unless they do. But Strauss's handling of the potentially explosive issue of electing twenty-five at-large members to the expanded Democratic National Committee suggests, at a minimum, that the Republicans should not assume a fragmented Democratic Party in the next presidential campaign.

The final slate of at-large candidates presented by Strauss in March 1973 and approved unanimously by the DNC's executive committee contained the personal choice of George Wallace, the personal choices of George Meany, and a sufficient number of labor leaders and others who had supported the 1972 presidential ticket to warrant the written endorsement of George McGovern. The feat required the most painstaking negotiations and a willingness to compromise on the part of all the contending parties. The National Committee adopted the slate without audible dissent.

Strauss regards elected Democratic officials—U.S. senators, House members, and governors, in particular—as his principal constituents, and it has been with their approval and support that he has gone about the thankless job of national chairman. Limited financing, as usual, will keep the National Committee from offering very much in the way of direct assistance to congressional or gubernatorial candidates in 1974. But Strauss will be working closely with the House and Senate campaign committees to do the best job they can in fund-raising and joint service projects for incumbent and nonincumbent candidates. There has been a generally good response from the McGovern mailing lists of 750,000 names that have now been made available to the National Committee.

Strauss's decision to go ahead with a second national telethon paid off handsomely, and he has also offered the first professional training school for potential Democratic candidates and their campaign directors. Under the chairmanship of Governor Jimmy Carter of Georgia, Strauss has organized a special campaign committee to coordinate the DNC's efforts to help candidates in 1974. If the Charter Commission were to

recommend a national financial structure, combined with a
year-round program of education, training, and campaign
services, these beginnings could become permanent features
of the DNC's political operations instead of the *ad hoc* mea-
sures they now are.

Statements on policy and ideology will come primarily from
the Democratic Advisory Council of Elected Officials, a clear
indication of Strauss's intention to take his principal cues
on such matters from public officeholders. Headed by the only
nonpublic official among its members, Arthur Krim of New
York, the council covers the political spectrum from Mc-
Govern to Wallace. More recently, the council has organized
specific task forces that include persons not holding public
office. The council has a great opportunity to begin the process
of evolving a new ideology for the Democrats, using its membership of governors, U.S. senators and representatives, mayors,
and other elected officials as national and regional spokesmen. The 1974 party conference offers an excellent forum for
the adoption of these positions by a truly representative assembly of the national Democratic Party. The council should
direct its energies in 1974 to drawing up an agenda of priority
issues for consideration and adoption by the conference.

GETTING THE MESSAGE THROUGH

Even if the Democrats are able to move away from their
preoccupation with internal reform and initiate a more
imaginative campaign on matters of public concern, they still
face the obstacle that traditionally confronts the party not
controlling the White House: How can the opposition party
effectively communicate with the voters?

President Nixon's persistent difficulties in communicating
effectively on the Watergate issue should not obscure the impact of his use of television and radio during most of his
Presidency. Nixon brought to a new level of intensity what
has been a traditional effort of all recent Presidents to over-
whelm the political opposition through the mass communications media. The scope of the Nixon effort was illustrated

by David S. Broder in a story in the *Washington Post* about elaborate preparations in early 1973 by the Nixon Administration's communications cadre to marshal public support for the President's position in a forthcoming battle with Congress over federal spending. According to Broder, public information officers from the federal agencies were summoned weekly to the Executive Office Building, adjacent to the White House, to report on their many assignments: scheduling at least three "budget" speeches a week for every political appointee in their agencies; delivering two signed editorial commentaries per week for placement in friendly newspapers; submitting articles to trade and business publications; scheduling frequent appearances by political appointees on local television and radio talk shows; and distributing canned radio tapes to local stations around the country. The White House closely supervised the content, suggesting key phrases and passages that made the President's point. As a morale-booster and reward for helping sustain Mr. Nixon's first veto of the session—the vocational rehabilitation legislation—the communications cadre received embossed presidential cufflinks from Ken Clawson, deputy director of communications for the executive branch, at their meeting on April 5.

"Mr. Nixon's men are organizing it with the same thoroughness—and many of the same techniques—they used in the last election campaign," Broder wrote. "In time, the 'selling of the budget' may make as striking a chapter in the public relations textbooks as the 'selling of the President.' "

Loud cries of outrage from Democrats on Capitol Hill, plus a report from the General Accounting Office pointing out that these activities were in violation of federal law prohibiting legislative lobbying with public funds, ended that particular operation. But it nevertheless symbolized the Nixon Administration's basic approach to public information or, as one less charitable might allege, political propaganda.

From the first moments of the Nixon Presidency, the media have received nonstop attention from scores—if not hundreds—of public relations types scattered throughout the White House and the executive agencies. Elaborate media advance work to ensure maximum local exposure precedes Cabinet officers whenever they travel. During his tenure as Communications Director for the Executive Branch, Herbert Klein set up regional briefings by the President for key editors and publishers. Spot guest appearances were arranged on the networks' most popular programs, from "Laugh-In" to Bob Hope specials and celebrity golf tournaments. Federal Communications Chairman Dean Burch telephoned network executives for transcripts of commentary following one of the President's televised messages on Vietnam. The "Dick Cavett Show" was told to invite an administration spokesman to defend the SST. Vice President Agnew took to the hustings to excoriate the *Washington Post,* the *New York Times,* and the network news organizations. Local groups of businessmen, known to be close supporters of Richard Nixon, challenged the license renewals of television stations owned by the *Washington Post.* Federal agencies saturated the mails with literature extolling the virtues of the Nixon Administration, all at taxpayer expense. The Justice Department attempted to subpoena the notes of newsmen and journalists. Public television fell into the iron grip of the White House, and offending programs were removed from the network. All in all, it has been an ambitious and well-rounded effort.

On the evening of the departure of the last POW from Vietnam, for example, President Nixon addressed the nation not only on the ending of that phase of American involvement in Indochina, but on a range of other topics as well: amnesty, meat prices, inflation generally, federal spending, the congressional response to his 1974 budget, military spending, and a direct appeal to the American people to flood the Congress with mail to support his expected vetoes. It was, by all odds, a cutting partisan speech that touched directly on a number of current political issues.

The next day Senator Mansfield and Speaker Albert informed the three television networks that Senator Muskie would deliver the Democratic reply in the Capitol at 9:30 P.M. the following Monday. They requested comparable live television coverage and, as usual, the three networks declined the request, although clips of the Muskie speech appeared on some network news programs. In a follow-up letter to the three network presidents, Senator Mansfield outlined his view of the consequences of their refusal to provide time for a full response:

> It has been estimated that 100 million people are watching television during prime time on a weekday, winter evening. When President Nixon is provided simultaneous coverage on all the networks, he speaks to 100 million people. There is no substitute for that type of total access to the American electorate. No amount of news shows individually aired can reach with such impact the American electorate; the characterization of events and issues in that forum has an impact on the perceptions of the issues that is difficult, if not impossible, to change. When the networks refuse to grant Congress an opportunity to communicate on the same scale as the President and the Executive, they are preventing Congress from fulfilling its co-equal role under the Constitution.

This is only one of the more recent examples of a problem that renders partially inoperable a basic assumption of the American political system: that the voter has a right to hear both sides of a political issue.

But, as someone always points out, the President has a right, even an obligation, to communicate with the people; and there is only one President. No one disputes this right or obligation. This presidential prerogative should not, however, be allowed to obscure an equally obvious need: for the major opposition party—whether Democratic or Republican—to have at least an occasional chance to reach the electorate with the scope and impact that are routinely guaranteed to the President. It is this opportunity that has been almost totally denied to the Democrats since 1969 and to the Republicans in the prior eight years.

During the national chairmanship of Lawrence F. O'Brien, in particular, the Democratic National Committee through its general counsel, Joseph A. Califano, Jr., attacked the problem of access to television and radio on three principal fronts:

(1) the paid-time cases wherein the DNC won a U.S. Court of Appeals decision that broadcasters cannot flatly refuse to sell time to the National Committee for fund-raising or the discussion of issues (a decision that obviously didn't get to the matter of whether the Democrats can afford to buy the time, or whether they should be forced to this expedient; in any event, the Supreme Court reversed the favorable Court of Appeals decision)

(2) the "fairness doctrine" cases wherein the DNC filed numerous complaints with the Federal Communications Commission and appeals to the federal courts following repeated denials by the networks of requests to respond to certain of President Nixon's televised messages

(3) the DNC's unsuccessful effort to persuade the FCC through its rule-making proceedings to redefine the obligation of broadcasters under the fairness doctrine to allow greater access to responsible parties to respond to presidential appearances

This comprehensive legal offensive produced very little. The Democrats did win a unanimous reversal by the U.S. Court of Appeals of an FCC order of August 1970 granting free broadcast time to the *Republican* National Committee to answer "The Democrats Respond: Part I," a thirty-minute program produced by the Democratic National Committee in July 1970 (free time that had been made available by CBS to respond, in part, to numerous broadcast appearances by President Nixon). The Court of Appeals not only turned down the Republicans but it sharply criticized the FCC for its "capricious, arbitrary and inconsistent approach to this case." Although that decision helped the Democrats only in a negative sense—that is, it kept the Republican spokesmen from getting even *more* broadcast time—it did open up the possibility that the networks might grant free time to the opposition party to answer the President without inevitably incurring the additional obligation then of giving time to the President's party.

But this victory did little to change the operational situation: President Nixon could appear on simultaneous network television whenever he wanted and say whatever struck his fancy, and the Democrats were routinely denied comparable time to respond. The denials by the networks, the FCC, and the federal courts follow a familiar litany: The fairness doctrine affords wide latitude to broadcasters in covering controversial issues of public importance, and a right of response to the President, as such, does not exist. Therefore, a broadcaster's obligation under the fairness doctrine can be discharged, for example, through a collection of thirty-second clips on the evening news; appearances on "Face the Nation," "Meet the Press," and "Issues and Answers"; and sporadic interviews on the "Today" show.

This rationale, however much it may accord with the legal subtleties of the fairness doctrine, fails to deal with the clear disparity between this kind of *ad hoc* exposure to a limited audience, filtered through a network news organization, and the impact of a sustained message, carried simultaneously on three networks, and expressed in a manner deemed by the opposition party to make its case most effectively. Until this disparity is explicitly recognized and positive steps are taken to do something about it, the endless rhetoric about the nuances of the fairness doctrine will remain what it is: fancy legal footwork that protects the President from his political opponents and relieves the networks of any continuing responsibility to provide a more equitable balance.

There are various ways to attack the problem. First, the FCC could redefine the broadcaster's obligation under the fairness doctrine along the lines advocated by the Democratic National Committee or some variation of its proposal. This would afford responsible opposition spokesmen "equal time" to respond to presidential addresses and news conferences carried on the broadcast media, although the right of reply would not necessarily be exercised in every instance by the opposition political party. Given the existing make-up of the FCC, there is little realistic hope that such a review of the fairness doctrine or a redefinition of its obligations will be forthcoming.

Second, the Congress could redefine the obligations of the

fairness doctrine through legislation. In 1970, for example, Senator Fulbright proposed a joint resolution that would require broadcasters to provide time to "authorized representatives" of the Senate and House, at least four times a year, to speak on public issues. The question of the fairness doctrine is, however, highly complicated, involving the access not only of Congress and the two major political parties but also of countless private groups that are contending for time on the public airwaves. As a consequence, there is great reluctance in Congress to open up the fairness doctrine issue to legislative solution, and the odds at present are very much against any such amendments to the Communications Act of 1934, especially since President Nixon would probably veto any bill that had the effect of giving his opposition greater access to the broadcast media.

Third, the networks could make available, on a voluntary basis, periodic opportunities for the opposition party to present its case to the viewers. There are precedents to support this approach: The networks now routinely provide free time each year for the opposition leaders in Congress to respond to the State of the Union message. If this is possible in January, it is hard to understand why comparable opportunities could not be offered at other times of the year.

In July 1970, CBS initiated what at first blush appeared to be a partial solution. Frank Stanton of CBS informed Democratic National Chairman O'Brien that the network planned to make available over the next year four thirty-minute time slots that could be used by the Democratic National Committee to respond to the Nixon Administration in whatever manner seemed most appropriate. The initial program, "The Democrats Respond: Part I," consisted of O'Brien answering a series of presidential statements covering a range of issues in what approximated a debate format. The resulting howls from the Republicans produced the litigation discussed above, but it also produced a decision by CBS to cancel the remaining three programs. Even though the Republicans' request for time was eventually denied by the U.S. Court of Appeals and the FCC was rebuked, CBS has been unwilling to reinstitute

"The Democrats Respond" series. Nor did the CBS offer resolve the problem of simultaneous coverage on all three networks.

More recently, CBS has experimented with offering various
persons an opportunity to comment briefly on presidential
addresses in place of their "instant analysis" by network cor-
respondents. This approach was not a conspicuous success,
and CBS abandoned it several months later. Senator Muskie
has proposed legislation that would provide the opposition
party's national committee with an automatic right of response whenever the President appeared on television or radio
within ten months of a presidential election and within
ninety days of congressional elections in nonpresidential years.
Others have proposed a series of "national debates" between
spokesmen for the national committees of the major parties to
be carried voluntarily by the commercial and public networks.

Congress, on its own initiative, could open the House and
Senate chambers to broadcast coverage. This reform would
provide a forum for the President's supporters as well as his
opponents, but it nevertheless would give the opposition party
leaders a much more effective way than now exists to respond
to presidential messages. For the Democratic majority in
Congress, a decision to open the legislative process to public
view would be an excellent way to demonstrate the party's
commitment to the Governing Issue. Experience with state
legislatures clearly suggests that the public is interested in
watching elected legislative bodies at work and that the resulting political benefits far outweigh the potential for embar-
rassment.

It comes down to how badly the Democrats want to get
their message through and how tough they want to get in
pursuing some greater degree of equity for the opposition
party. The levers of power exist in Congress, if the Democrats
can reach a decision to pull them.

NOTES

CHAPTER 1. POLITICS AND THE PRESIDENCY

1. This section of Chapter 1 draws heavily upon the data of Albert H. Cantril and Charles W. Roll, Jr., as contained in "That Landslide Was No Mandate," "Outlook" section, *The Washington Post,* December 10, 1972. I am indebted to them for permission to use these data.

2. Unofficial election returns show the following popular vote percentages:

	Democratic	Republican	Other
33 states having senatorial races:			
Presidential vote	36.9%	63.0%	0.1%
Senatorial vote	46.1	53.5	0.4
18 states having gubernatorial races:			
Presidential vote	36.3%	63.4%	0.3%
Gubernatorial vote	49.6	49.7	0.7

3. Interviewing was subcontracted to the Gallup Organization. I am grateful for permission to report these findings.

4. V. O. Key, Jr., *The Responsible Electorate: Rationality in Presidential voting, 1936–1960* (Cambridge, Mass. The Belknap Press, 1966), pp. 61–62.

5. Two studies, in January 1971 and June 1972, reported that the great majority of Americans had a healthy sense of their personal progress and looked optimistically to the future. See Albert H. Cantril and Charles W. Roll, Jr., *Hopes and Fears of the American People* (New York: Universe Books, 1971), and William Watts and Lloyd A. Free, *State of the Nation* (New York: Uni-

verse Books, 1972). In fact, Watts and Free reported that Americans "tended to be even more optimistic about their personal futures in mid–1972 than they had been a year and a half before."

6. These data are reported in Arthur H. Miller, "Political Issues and Trust in Government: 1964–1970," a paper prepared for delivery at the American Political Science Association, 1972, p. 3.

7. These results are from a study conducted for the American Federation of State, County, and Municipal Employees. Interviewing was subcontracted to the Gallup Organization. I am grateful to AFSCME for permission to report these data.

8. For a discussion along these lines, see Miller, "Political Issues and Trust," pp. 30–49.

9. Gary Warren Hart, *Right from the Start: A Chronicle of the McGovern Campaign* (New York: Quadrangle, 1973), pp. 266–67, 285–86.

10. For an excellent discussion of the McGovern campaign and its effects on the Democratic Party, see Ted Van Dyk, "The Hero of a Year Ago," *The Washington Monthly*, Vol. 5, No. 3 (May, 1973), pp. 39–46.

CHAPTER 2.   THE REFORM IMPERATIVE

1. Statistics on the composition of the 1968 and 1972 Democratic National Conventions are drawn from *Mandate for Reform: A Report of the Commission on Party Structure and Delegate Selection* (Washington: Democratic National Committee, 1970), and from a report, "The Delegates of '72," prepared by Martin Plissner, political editor, CBS News.

2. *Call to Order: A Narrative Report by the Commission on Rules of the Democratic National Committee* (Washington: Democratic National Committee, 1972), p. 11.

3. *The Presidential Nominating Conventions 1968* (Washington: Congressional Quarterly Service, 1968), p. 201.

4. *Ibid.*, pp. 194–95.

5. *Mandate for Reform,* p. 49.

6. Frederick G. Dutton, *Changing Sources of Power: American Politics in the 1970s* (New York: McGraw-Hill, 1971), p. 26.

7. The high showing of McGovern among registered 18-to-24-year-olds is explained by the strong preference in the spring of college students for McGovern and the fact that there are twice as many college students who are registered as unregistered:

	Nixon	McGovern	Undecided
College	35%	61%	4%
Noncollege	48	44	8

8. The eighteen guidelines are contained in *Mandate for Reform*, pp. 33–48.

9. *Ibid.*, p. 49.

10. One of the commission's more curious decisions was its total reliance on "state parties" in implementing the eighteen guidelines. Once the contest for the nomination is under way, the presidential contenders, not the state parties, are the principal actors in the delegate-selection process and the ones who bear major responsibility for observing the rules. Prior to this time, of course, the state parties had the job of approving the rules or amending state laws to comply with the standards that had been established.

11. It was also a departure from the agreement reached between the major Democratic contenders and Democratic National Chairman Lawrence F. O'Brien to "eschew frivolous challenges" and to refrain from using "credentials challenges as a tactic in pursuit of delegate support." The agreement was signed on July 14, 1971, in Washington, D.C.

12. Speech by Louis Harris, National Press Club, Washington, D.C., November 10, 1972, p. 17.

13. Representative James G. O'Hara suggested the term "casual Democrats."

14. *Call to Order*, pp. 49–51.

15. James G. O'Hara, "The New Convention," *FACT*, October 29, 1971, p. 2.

16. The only major exception to this conclusion arose out of the dispute over the number of delegate votes that would constitute a majority in settling the South Carolina and California credentials challenges on the convention floor. Temporary Convention Chairman Lawrence F. O'Brien ruled that the 151 challenged California delegates could not vote on any roll call involving that challenge and that not 1,509 (an absolute majority of the 3,016 delegate votes) but a simple majority of those *eligible* to vote would be sufficient to decide the challenges. This ruling was bitterly opposed by the Humphrey, Muskie, Jackson, Mills, and Wallace forces, who argued that an absolute majority was required and charged that O'Brien had capitulated to the

McGovern forces. O'Brien took the position that the rules clearly stated that a delegate could not vote on his or her challenge and that permitting the 151 challenged California delegates to vote would be tantamount to giving them an automatic "no" vote at the outset. In the end, both the South Carolina and California challenges were decided by more than the absolute majority of 1,509 (the McGovern forces lost South Carolina and won California), so the impact of O'Brien's ruling remains speculative. Some persons contend it effectively gave the nomination to McGovern; others argue that McGovern had already secured sufficient votes to win the nomination regardless of the ruling.

17. *Life,* July 7, 1972, p. 31.

CHAPTER 3.

DEMOCRATS WHO WEREN'T SUPPOSED TO WIN BUT DID

1. In five states the two houses would be controlled by opposite parties, and in two states there would be a tie in one house of the legislature.

2. See Chapter 1, page 21.

3. The most striking age differential of all occurred in Democratic primary contests for the House. The six Democratic incumbents who were defeated for renomination averaged 71.6 years of age, compared to 35.8 years for the successful challengers. Three of these primary winners, however, went on to lose to older Republicans in the general election.

4. The trend toward youthful victory in congressional races was not the sole preserve of the Democrats. In their five victories over Democratic incumbents in the House, the winning GOP challengers averaged 31.8 years of age compared to 57.7 years for the losing Democrats. In the two races where Republicans captured governorships previously controlled by Democrats, the winners—Holshouser of North Carolina, thirty-seven, and Bond of Missouri, thirty-three—were, again, considerably younger than their Democratic opponents, who were fifty-two and fifty-four years old, respectively. The pattern did not hold, however, in the four Senate races where Republicans captured previously Democratic seats: One Republican was younger, two were older, and one was the same age.

5. The voter identification system was designed and supervised by Valentine-Sherman Associates of Minneapolis, Minnesota.

6. Federal Communications Commissioner Nicholas Johnson, a native of Iowa, had earlier given serious thought to running for the Democratic Senate nomination, but he, too, decided against it.

7. In addition to Clark's victory, the number of Democrats in the state legislature was increased by 50 per cent and the Democrats picked up another seat in the House of Representatives. Outside of the presidential contest, 1972 was a banner year for Iowa Democrats.

8. Allott received 51 per cent in 1954, 53 per cent in 1960 and 58 per cent in 1966.

9. Much of the information relating to the Young campaign was prepared by Stuart E. Eizenstat and William B. Barutio, both of Atlanta, for their analysis, "Andrew Young: The Path to History."

10. Senator McGovern lost the 5th district by 3,443 votes.

CHAPTER 4. COALITION AND IDEOLOGY: LEGACY OF PARADOX

1. For an excellent critique of the Phillips analysis, see Nelson W. Polsby and Aaron B. Wildavsky, *Presidential Elections* (New York: Charles Scribner's Sons, 1971), pp. 89–93.

2. Key, *Responsible Electorate*, pp. 7, 30.

3. These data are from pre- and post-election surveys by the Gallup Poll.

4. Again, these data are from the Gallup Poll.

5. The Gallup data upon which these differences are based are:

	1939			1973		
	Dem.	Rep.	Ind.	Dem.	Rep.	Ind.
East	33%	42%	25%	41%	27%	32%
Midwest	38	42	20	36	31	33
South	70	20	10	47	22	31
West	45	34	21	46	27	27

6. Gallup data for these differences are:

	1939			1973		
	Dem.	Rep.	Ind.	Dem.	Rep.	Ind.
Prof. and business	29%	46%	25%	32%	32%	36%
White collar	40	36	24	33	32	35
Manual worker	46	34	20	46	20	34
Farmer	49	38	13	41	32	27

7. Hart, *Right from Start,* p. 328.
8. The question asked: "How would you describe yourself—as very conservative, fairly conservative, middle-of-the-road, fairly liberal, or very liberal?"
9. Walter Dean Burnham, in *National Observer,* November 18, 1972, p. 30.
10. For a description of the ideological battery of questions, see Lloyd A. Free and Hadley Cantril, *The Political Beliefs of Americans* (New Brunswick, N.J.: Rutgers University Press, 1968), pp. 24–32, 209–10.
11. *Ibid.,* pp. 13–15, 207–8.
12. *Ibid.,* p. 32. For scoring of these indices, see p. 207.
13. *Ibid.,* p. 37.
14. *Ibid.,* p. 40.
15. I am indebted to Albert H. Cantril and Charles W. Roll, Jr., of the Gallup organization, for assistance in the design and execution of this survey.
16. Watts and Free, *State of the Nation,* pp. 294–97.
17. *Ibid.,* pp. 221–22.
18. *Ibid.,* p. 299.
19. I am indebted to Charles W. Roll, Jr., for his imaginative wording of this question.
20. The following areas were seen primarily as responsibilities of the federal government: national defense, social security, cancer research, pollution control, drug reform, prison reform, health insurance, and welfare. State and local governments were seen to hold primary responsibility for transportation, housing, and education.
21. The late Morton Grodzins of the University of Chicago was the pioneer in developing this understanding of the American federal system.
22. Burnham in *National Observer,* November 18, 1972.
23. This point is discussed by Elinor Graham in "The Politics of Poverty," in Marvin E. Gettleman and David Mermelstein, eds.,

The Great Society Reader: The Failure of American Liberalism
(New York: Random House, 1967), pp. 213–16.

24. Watts and Free, *State of the Nation*, p. 25.
25. Richard M. Scammon and Ben J. Wattenberg, *The Real Majority: An Extraordinary Examination of the American Electorate* (New York: Coward-McCann, 1970), p. 30.
26. *Ibid.*, p. 81.
27. U.S. Congress, Senate, Subcommittee on Intergovernmental Relations, *Confidence and Concern: Citizens View American Government* (93d Cong., 1st Sess., 1973), pp. v–vii, 49.
28. Watts and Free, *State of the Nation.* © 1973 by Potomac Associates, Washington, D.C. P. 192.

CHAPTER 5. COALITION AND IDEOLOGY: PERSPECTIVE OF THE '70s

1. See Michael Barone, "The Gains of Landslide Losers," "Outlook" section, *The Washington Post,* April 1, 1973, p. C1.
2. *Ibid.*, p. C1.
3. I am indebted to Albert H. Cantril for stressing this point.
4. Watts and Free, *State of the Nation,* pp. 270–71.
5. *Ibid.*, p. 251.
6. *Ibid.*, p. 269.
7. William F. Buckley, Jr., *Up from Liberalism* (New York: Bantam edition, 1968), p. xxi.
8. Alice M. Rivlin, "A Counter-Budget for Social Progress," *New York Times Magazine,* April 8, 1973, pp. 33, 84.
9. Henry Fairlie, *The Kennedy Promise: The Politics of Expectation* (New York: Doubleday, 1973), pp. 11–12.
10. The reader is urged to see Gettleman and Mermelstein, eds., *Great Society Reader.*
11. Michael Novak, "Notes for a New Democratic Realism," *Commonweal,* March 23, 1973, p. 71.
12. See Richard Cornuelle, *Reclaiming the American Dream* (New York: Random House, 1965).
13. Rivlin, "A Counter-Budget," p. 95.

INDEX